AROUND A THIN PLACE

An Iona pilgrimage guide

AROUND A THIN PLACE

An Iona pilgrimage guide

Jane Bentley and Neil Paynter

WILD GOOSE PUBLICATIONS

CONTENTS

INTRODUCTION

For centuries, millennia even, Iona has drawn travellers to it in search of the sacred. This quest for the holy runs as a common thread all the way from ancient times to the 6th-century voyage of Saint Columba – and to today's pilgrims who arrive on the jetty from every corner of the world. George MacLeod, the Founder of the Iona Community, described the island as a 'thin place' – only a 'tissue paper' separating the material from the spiritual.

The Iona Community has for many years run a weekly pilgrimage around the island, stopping at places of significance – be they historical, religious, or simply thought-provoking. The Iona Community's witness of perceiving a close connection between the spiritual and the material is reflected in the pilgrimage: one stop may take prayerful inspiration from Columban times, while another highlights the struggle for justice and peace in the developing world.

The pilgrimage is led by staff from the Abbey and MacLeod Centre, and is never the same twice. Each person brings their own unique understanding and perspective. Lurking in the Community office is a battered ring-binder representing the contributions of past pilgrimage leaders – packed to overflowing with prayers and poems, either copied or self-penned, songs, historical titbits, reflections and stories. It has been the direct inspiration for this book.

Our hope is that in collating some of these resources, they will offer inspiration and reflective possibilities not only for those who seek to conduct their own pilgrimages around the island, but also for 'armchair pilgrims' who may not be able to visit Iona in person. We've even included the Abbey kitchen's recipe for flapjack (delivered to the Machair with a hot cup of tea on pilgrimage days) – if you want to really recreate the experience!

How to use this book

Just as the original ring-binder is a work in progress, this book is offered as a menu of possibilities, rather than as a definitive guide. For each stop we have included an introduction giving some background to the stop, followed by a Bible reading, some additional resources such as reflections, poems and prayers, and suggestions for songs. It would certainly become a penitential pilgrimage if all of these resources were used at each stop – please simply pick what is useful for you.

We have also included a blank page after the stops, so that you can continue the 'work in progress' by adding your own pilgrimage inspirations. These might be in the form of prayers, pictures, jotted thoughts, stories, memories … Pat Bennett, a member of the Iona Community who has been on many a pilgrimage, offers the following idea:

Whilst on assorted pilgrimages through Japan in the 17th century, the Zen monk Matsuo Basho distilled the essence of what he saw, smelled and touched, the conversations and encounters of his journeys, and the deeper mysteries he sensed through all of these, into various poetic forms. Whilst writing haiku (a three-line poem of 5, 7 and 5 syllables respectively) is not necessarily everyone's forte, I've found that the process of trying to identify and articulate a key element from each of the stops en route around the island can be a really helpful way of focussing my thoughts, and of translating the pilgrimage experience from being merely (!) a very enjoyable and informative amble round the island, into a richly rewarding and sometimes life-changing journey. At each stopping place, I try to pick up one thing – maybe a phrase or a particular image – from the talk/meditation/prayer that is offered, and then, for at least part of the walk to the next station, turn it over in my mind and search for the heart of it. There seems to be something about the rhythm of walking itself which is very conducive to this sort of rumination. I'll try (or at least begin) to compose and scribble down a short prayer or meditation, a single sentence or maybe even a haiku, to capture and contain this insight so that I can remember it and return to it later for further thought.

A series of Pat's reflective Iona haiku can be found on page 166.

A note about safety

There are two pilgrimages described in this book – the 'off-road' and the 'on-road'. The off-road pilgrimage is a walk of nearly seven miles over boggy and rocky terrain. Strong footwear and waterproof clothing are essential, along with food and drink for the journey. We have included a map, but have left it very basic to encourage you to travel with a proper, detailed map – people have lost their lives by simply heading off to explore the island, and even broken limbs may require a helicopter airlift to hospital in Glasgow – not the best way to remember Iona. Even pilgrimage leaders can get lost – as Brian Woodcock describes on page 51.

Not everyone has the mobility to be able to undertake such a journey, and it is not intended as a form of penance! Some years ago, the weekly pilgrimages were returning hours late, as increasingly infirm participants engaged in heroic struggles to complete the walk. We also had to continually disappoint people who turned up in more 'urban' footwear, which would not allow them to walk in safety. To this end, the on-road pilgrimage was devised to allow as many people as possible to participate and still feel part of a real pilgrimage. This forms the second half of this book, and includes many of the stops from the off-road pilgrimage (which are referenced by page number).

At the time of printing, the Iona Community runs both pilgrimages on a Tuesday. They are open to the public, with the off-road version departing at roughly 10.15am, and the on-road at noon. See www.iona.org.uk for the Iona Community's contact details.

Blessed journeys!

Thank you

Thank you to everyone who contributed to this book, especially Rowena Aberdeen, Pat Bennett, Lisa Bodenheim, Ruth Burgess, Nancy Cocks, David Coleman, Anja Grosse-Uhlmann, Michelle Harris, Chris Redhead, Anikó Schuetz, Jan Sutch Pickard, Lotte Webb and Brian Woodcock. Thank you also to Jane Darroch Riley for the beautiful design and layout. And Neil and Jane wish to warmly thank each other.

KEY TO MAP

1. St Martin's Cross/Reilig Odhráin
2. The Nunnery/Village
3. Crossroads
4. The Marble Quarry
5. St Columba's Bay
6. Loch Staonaig
7. The Machair
8. Hill of the Angels
9. The Hermit's Cell
10. Dun I
11. Dunsmeorach
12. Parish Church/MacLean's Cross
13. The Jetty/Martyrs' Bay
14. Erratic boulder
15. The House of Prayer

MAP OF IONA

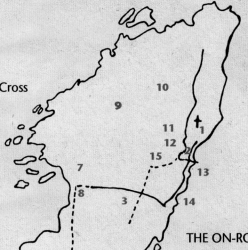

THE OFF-ROAD PILGRIMAGE

St Martin's Cross
The Nunnery
Crossroads
High point
The Marble Quarry
St Columba's Bay
Loch Staonaig
The Machair
Hill of the Angels
The Hermit's Cell
Dun I
Reilig Odhráin

THE ON-ROAD PILGRIMAGE

St Martin's Cross
Dunsmeorach
Parish Church
MacLean's Cross
The Nunnery
The Jetty
Martyrs' Bay
Erratic boulder
Crossroads
The Machair
Hill of the Angels
The House of Prayer
The Village
Reilig Odhráin

To get to Iona

To get to Iona
it takes me
the Underground
three trains
a coach
two ferries
and a fair bit of walking.

To get to Iona
it takes me
sandwiches
coffee
sweets
a bottle of water
and sometimes
on the boat
an egg-and-bacon butty.

To get to Iona
it takes me
timetables
The Guardian quick crossword
a book
a pen and some paper
and whatever magazines
people leave behind them
on the trains.

To get to Iona
it takes me
smiles
conversations
laughter
listening
memories
and often tears.

To get to Iona
it takes me
risks
prayers
work
wonder
minutes and days
and the passing of years.

That's what it takes me
to get to Iona.

What will it take you?

Ruth Burgess

THE OFF-ROAD PILGRIMAGE

ST MARTIN'S CROSS

St Martin of Tours lived about two hundred years before St Columba, in the fourth century. He was named after Mars, the Roman god of war, and came from a military family; and so, he spent his early years living the life of a Roman soldier.

Legend has it that, one day on garrison duty, he met a beggar outside a city gate. It was a deathly cold day and the homeless man was shivering and dressed in rags. The naked suffering of the poor man suddenly touched Martin's heart, and, moved with compassion, he stripped off his military cloak, which was lined with thick lamb's wool, cut it in half with his soldier's sword and shared it with the homeless man. That night, Martin had a dream of Jesus, surrounded by saints and angels, and wearing the coat he had given to the beggar.

Martin continued in the military life. Until one night, just before a major battle, he reported to his generals, and informed them that he could no longer serve. 'I am a soldier of Christ: I cannot fight,' he confessed.

Martin dedicated the rest of his life to the ministry of hospitality, good works, and evangelism, playing a prominent role in the mission to the Celts.

St Martin's Cross has been rooted here, in its original spot, for over 1200 years – through Viking raids, the Middle Ages, the Renaissance, the Age of Reason, the industrial revolution, the world wars, the Cold War … A modern-day pilgrim to Iona wrote: 'St Martin's Cross stands as a constant witness to the timelessness and faithfulness of God against the ever-changing sky and the passing centuries.'

Carved on the east face of St Martin's Cross are jewel-like bosses and an interweaving Celtic pattern, symbolic of the intertwining of earth and heaven, the sacred and the secular. George MacLeod, the Founder of the Iona Community, famously said of Iona: 'Iona is a very thin place. There is only a tissue-paper layer between things material and things spiritual.' On the west side of the cross are scenes from the Bible: Daniel in the lion's den, Abraham and Isaac, David playing the harp, the Virgin and Child …

St Martin's life – like our own unpredictable lives – was an amazing journey of straight roads, sudden life-changing encounters, crossroads of indecision, complete turnarounds, new horizons …

Think for a moment about your own life journey up until now … And of those you journey alongside today: friends and strangers on this pilgrimage; companions on the road of life; brothers and sisters in the wider world, with whom we share this precious planet. We are all interconnected and held in God's hand.

BIBLE READINGS

Then the king will say to those at his right hand, 'Come, you that are blessed by my Father, inherit the kingdom prepared for you from the foundation of the world; for I was hungry and you gave me food, I was thirsty and you gave me something to drink, I was a stranger and you welcomed me, I was naked and you gave me clothing, I was sick and you took care of me, I was in prison and you visited me.' Then the righteous will answer him, 'Lord, when was it that we saw you hungry and gave you food, or thirsty and gave you something to drink? And when was it that we saw you a stranger and welcomed you, or naked and gave you clothing? And when was it that we saw you sick or in prison and visited you?'

And the king will answer them, 'Truly I tell you, just as you did it to one of the least of these who are members of my family, you did it to me.'

Matthew 25:34–40 (NRSV)

Leviticus 26:12
Micah 6:8
John 14:4–6

REFLECTIONS

Setting out on the road ...

Setting out is first of all getting out of ourself. Breaking through the shell of selfishness hardening us within our own ego.

To stop revolving round ourself as if we were the centre of everything.

Refusing to be ringed in by the problems of our own small world. However important these may be, humanity is more important and our task is to serve humanity.

Setting out is not covering miles of land or sea, or travelling faster than the speed of sound. It is first and foremost opening ourselves to other people, trying to get to know them, going out to meet them.

Opening ourselves to ideas, including those with which we disagree, this is what the good traveller should do. Happy are they who understand the words: 'If you disagree with me, you have something to give me.'

If those who are with you always agree with you before you open your mouth, they are not companions but shadows. When disagreement is not a form of systematic blocking, when it rises from a different vision, it can only enrich us.

It is possible to travel alone. But the good traveller knows that the journey is human life and life needs company. 'Companion' means ... the one who eats the same bread. Happy are they who feel they are always on the road and everyone they meet is their chosen companion. The good traveller takes care of weary companions. They guess when they lose heart. They take them as they find them, listen to them. Intelligently, gently, above all lovingly, they encourage them to go on and recover their joy in the journey.

To travel for the sake of travelling is not the true journey. We must seek a goal, envisage an end to the journey, an arrival.

But there are journeys and journeys. For the Abrahamic minorities, setting out means to get moving and help many others get moving to make the world juster and more human.

Dom Helder Camara (adapted)

The call

As Jesus walked along the shore of the Lake of Galilee, he saw two brothers, Simon (called Peter) and his brother Andrew, casting a net into the lake; for they were fishermen.

Matthew 4:18

The two characters stand apart from each other, Peter looking quite absorbed in himself.

Jesus:	Peter ...?
Peter:	Yes, Jesus ...?
Jesus:	Come with me.
Peter:	Where are you going?
Jesus:	I'm not telling you.
Peter:	Do you not know?
Jesus:	Oh yes, I've a fair idea.
Peter:	Then ... why won't you tell me?
Jesus:	You might not like it.
Peter:	Well, thanks for your consideration, Jesus.
	(A pause)
Jesus:	Peter ...?
Peter:	Yes, Jesus ...?

Jesus: Come with me.

Peter: Can I bring somebody else?

Jesus: Just bring yourself.

Peter: Will there only be the two of us?

Jesus: Oh no, there'll be plenty of others.

Peter: Will I know some of them?

                  What about my cousin Alec …
                  will he be there?

                  And is there any chance of my sister coming
                  if she still fancies you?

                  And what about my gran?
                  Oh, Jesus, I'd love to bring my gran to meet you.
                  Can I?

Jesus: Peter … just bring yourself.

Peter: But … but … you said there would be others.

Jesus: That's right.

Peter: Who are they?

Jesus: I'm not telling you.

Peter:	Why not?
Jesus:	You might not like them.
Peter:	Aw, thanks a bunch, Jesus!
	(A pause)
Jesus:	Peter …?
Peter:	Yes, Jesus???
Jesus:	Come with me.
Peter:	Jesus, I've got better things to do than go on a mystery tour. But I'll think about it. Just tell me what I'll need.
Jesus:	What do you mean?
Peter:	Well, if I'm going somewhere I don't know, with people you refuse to tell me about, there are some things that might come in very handy.
Jesus:	Like what?
Peter:	Like something to read in case I get bored … Like something to sing in case I get sad … Like a new pair of jeans in case there's a dance or a party!

Jesus:	Peter, you'll not need anything. Just bring yourself. That's enough to contend with.
Peter:	Jesus … do you want me to end up like you???
Jesus:	Peter … I'm going … Are you coming with me?

Wild Goose Resource Group

PRAYERS

A heart willing to serve

Lord God, King of the universe,
who called Martin from military service
to follow in the way of Christ:
give us, we pray, the grace of compassion
and a heart willing to serve,
that we may respond to you
in the needs of others,
through Jesus Christ, your Son, our Lord.

Author unknown

St Martin's Cross

In the intertwining of my life with yours
brokenness meets re-making.

In the intertwining of my life with yours
restlessness meets peace.

In the intertwining of my life with yours
bondage meets liberation.

In the intertwining of my life with yours
weakness meets strength.

In the intertwining of my life with yours
selfishness meets servanthood.

In the intertwining of my life with yours
death meets resurrection.

In the intertwining of my life with yours
your kingdom comes.

Pat Bennett

Blessing

Bless to us, O God, the earth beneath our feet.
Bless to us, O God, the path whereon we go.
Bless to us, O God, the people whom we meet.
Bless to us, O God, each thing our eyes see.
Bless to us, O God, each sound our ears hear.
Bless to us, O God, each ray that guides our way.
Amen

A Celtic blessing

SONGS

I was hungry (*We Walk His Way*, Wild Goose Publications)
Siyahamba (We are marching in the light of God) (*Freedom Is Coming*, WGP)

ON THE WAY

Disturber

Disturbing stranger,
you call and we follow.
You call, and we leave behind
the nets of our past lives;
the things that bound and held us;
our old selves and our regrets.

For calling and disturbing,
for surprising and making new,
for moving us towards wholeness,
we thank you Lord.

Kate McIlhagga

NUNNERY

The Nunnery was founded by the Augustinians in the early 13th century, at about the same time as the Benedictine abbey was built. However, they are in very different states today. The abbey has been rebuilt, while the nunnery stands in ruins, with half-fallen walls and rooms open to the sky, and a garden where the cloisters once stood. Ironically, though, these remains are said to be one of the best-preserved medieval nunneries in the British Isles.

It was home to a working community until the latter part of the 16th century, and the nuns' pattern of daily life would have been very similar to that of the monks: eating their meals together in the refectory, worshipping in the chapel and going about their everyday tasks. They offered 400 years of service but we know next to nothing about them. In some ways, this can be seen as a reflection of church life down through the centuries, where men have primarily held positions of authority and women have been relegated to the periphery. There were once plans to rebuild the Nunnery, but perhaps the ruins are more evocative, and act as a reminder of the often overlooked role of women.

If you pause for a minute to reflect on church history, many more male than female names spring to mind. So it is here that we pause to remember women of faith – women whose lives we do know about from ages past – such as the Woman at the Well, the Samaritan woman, Saints Hildegard, Julian and Bridget – as well as more recent figures, such as Dorothy Day, Rosa Parks, Mother Teresa … Let us also remember those women whose names never made the history books; as well as the countless contemporary women who shape the world through their service, and yet go largely unnoticed. Let us remember the women who have influenced our own lives by their example. And if you wish, speak any of these names aloud now, so that these nunnery walls may once again reverberate with the energy of women who have served God …

(Brief pause during which people can speak names aloud; it can help if one of the pilgrimage leaders starts.)

Let us give thanks for their lives and witness. Amen

BIBLE READINGS

While Jesus was in Bethany in the home of Simon the Leper, a woman came to him with an alabaster jar of very expensive perfume, which she poured on his head as he was reclining at the table.

When the disciples saw this, they were indignant. 'Why this waste?' they asked. 'This perfume could have been sold at a high price and the money given to the poor.'

Aware of this, Jesus said to them, 'Why are you bothering this woman? She has done a beautiful thing to me. The poor you will always have with you, but you will not always have me. When she poured this perfume on my body, she did it to prepare me for burial. Truly I tell you, wherever this gospel is preached throughout the world, what she has done will also be told, in memory of her.'

Matthew 26:6–13 (NIV)

John 4:5–40
John 8:1–11

REFLECTIONS

The Abbess's farewell

It is the end.
The last evening on Columcille's Isle,
before the sword, the killing comes.
We three, who alone remain of our ancient sisterhood,
will make ready our few possessions,
the Word of God,
the cup of blessing,
our salves,
some food.

Then, shawl-clad,
in the wool from mountain sheep we've tended,
we'll row away from Iona of our hearts,
Iona of our love,
and in a far-off cave we'll sit,
and pray,
and think on what is to come.

Who will remember our sisterhood?
Shall we be minded on?
For eons our joys, our lives,
have been a living witness
to God's presence,
in the rocks and stones,
in the wildness of the waves and winds,
the lonely hillsides.

As our Brothers followed Colum's hallowed memory,
and Adomnán's Rule,

we sisters,
faithful to the Triune God of Wisdom, Love and Justice,
opened our doors to the orphaned child,
broken men,
and homeless women.

We gave refuge to the wounded soldier fleeing battle,
to the violated girl whose child we'd love,
through tending plants we sought the earth's healing wisdom.

And all the time we listened,
listened to the heartbeat of God,
whose name is Justice.

And shall we be remembered?

It may be that the very stones enshrine our prayers,
our hopes,
our dreams.

It may be that when pilgrims come to Colum's blessed Isle,
that they will stop,
and pause amid our ruined stones,
and know that veilèd sisters lived a ministry,
faithful to God's little ones,
and faithful to this sacred earth.

And let them know that in the presence of the Triune three,
of Wisdom, Love and Justice,
our sisterhood prays on, dreams on, that the pilgrims find peace.
My sisters, let us go.

Mary Grey

God and man and woman

A: In the beginning, God made man.
He was so disappointed that he tried again,

and the next time, he made woman.

B: Eve, the first woman, was a vegetarian.
She liked apples, and ate the wrong one.

Men have been suspicious of vegetarians ever since.

A: Noah didn't eat apples.
He was a man … so he drank alcohol.
In fact, he drank so much alcohol that one day
his sons found their old man completely sozzled
and lying in the nude.

Women have been suspicious of alcohol ever since.

B: Lot didn't eat apples or drink wine.
He just lived in a city where the men didn't know who they fancied.
So God told him to leave the city, and so he did.
God said, 'Don't look back, for I'm going to burn down the city.'
So Lot didn't look back, but his wife did
and she turned into a pillar of salt.

Women have never looked back since.

A: Delilah didn't eat apples, drink wine or look back.
She was a hairdresser.
Samson didn't know that,
but while he was resting his macho muscles,
Delilah cut his hair and took his strength away.

Men have avoided being bald ever since.

B: St Paul didn't know Eve, Noah, Lot or Delilah.
But he did know some women,
and those he did must have given him bad memories.
Because he told them not to speak in church,
not to go into church without a hat
and always to obey their husbands.
Paul also said that men shouldn't get married
unless they were able to control themselves.

Men have been unable to control themselves ever since.

A: But Jesus was different.

He was strong, but he cried.
He even cried in front of other men.
He knew that some women had bad reputations,
but that didn't keep him back from them:
he knelt beside them.

He loved his disciples who were all men
and he wasn't afraid to tell them that he loved them.
And though he was never married,
he was always surrounded by women, who, at his death,
were more faithful to him than the men.

Jesus didn't make a fuss about who was who, or who was what.
He said that everyone who loved him was his mother,
his sister,
his brother.

A&B: Thank God for Jesus.

Wild Goose Resource Group

The Nunnery in winter

The walls of my house
lie fallen
the stones mumbling
a litany of brokenness.

Yet, defying winter's imperious logic,
the vivid beauty of a few late flowers
clinging in the crevices
seems a sign that
you at least
still hope.

And I take it as a pledge
that together
from these ruins
we will fashion new things.

Pat Bennett

PRAYER

Lord of the excluded,
open my ears to those I would prefer not to hear;
open my life to those I would prefer not to know;
open my heart to those I would prefer not to love;
and so open my eyes to see
where I exclude You.

Pat Bennett

SONGS

Let's walk together (Sarantañani) (*Sent by the Lord*, WGP)
Ukrainian kyrie (*Many and Great*, Wild Goose Publications)

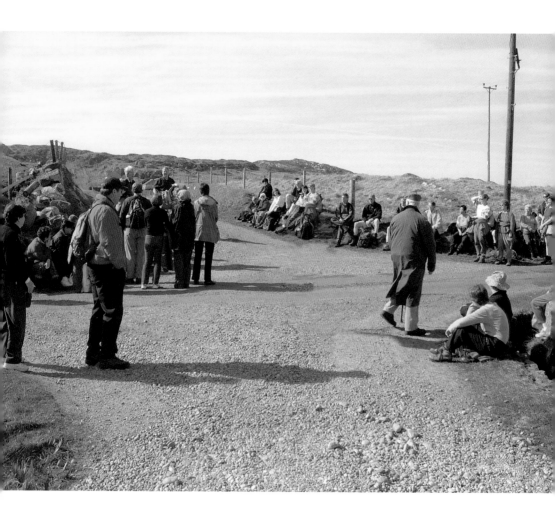

CROSSROADS

This is the only crossroads on Iona, somewhat ambitiously known as the 'four roads' (whereas to the untrained eye, it looks more like the intersection of a road and a track). Up until the earlier part of the 19th century, when the island's population peaked at over 500 people, it would have been a place of communication, of meeting and sharing news and gossip.

On the pilgrimage, it is a place of decisions: of whether to take the rough, boggy track up the hill towards the Marble Quarry, or the more gentle road to the Machair. Sometimes it is a hard decision to make, as we weigh up our desire to do the 'whole' pilgrimage with our capacity to do so, and the capability of our footwear.

Here, we also pause to remember the crossroads in our own life journeys, where our decisions may take us down new and unfamiliar paths.

We also remember places and people at a crossroads in their history. George MacLeod prayed that God would take us 'outside holiness, out to where soldiers curse and nations clash at the crossroads of the world'.

He writes:

'I simply argue that the cross be raised again
at the centre of the market place
as well as on the steeple of the church.
I am recovering the claim
that Jesus was not crucified in a cathedral
between two candles,
but on a cross between two thieves;
on the town garbage heap;
at a crossroad so cosmopolitan
that they had to write his title in Hebrew
and in Latin and in Greek (or shall we say

in English, in Bantu and in Afrikaans!);
at the kind of place where cynics talk smut,
and thieves curse, and soldiers gamble.
Because that is where he died.
And that is what he died about.
And that is where the church should be
and what the church should be about.'

From Only One Way Left

BIBLE READINGS

This is what the Lord says:
'Stand at the crossroads and look;
ask for the ancient paths,
ask where the good way is, and walk in it,
and you will find rest for your souls.'

Jeremiah 6:16 (NIV)

Psalm 23
Isaiah 42:16

PRAYER

Living God,
our journey in life is straightforward,
for most of us, most of the time.
We all jog along together
without having to think very much about it.
But then, suddenly, we find ourselves at a crossroads.

And we wonder where we should go next.
And nothing is clear at all.

Crossroads are places where we must make decisions
and choose which route to take.
They can be painful places, and places where sacrifices have to be made.
They can also be places of liberation.
For Jesus, the place of the cross was all of those things.

At this place, we think of people we know
who are at a crossroads,
and we hold them in our prayers.

And we ask that,
wherever we are in our journey,
we may take the path that is right for us
and for those with whom we travel.

Brian Woodcock

SONGS

Bless the Lord, my soul (Taizé)
Take, O take me as I am (*Come All You People*, Wild Goose Publications)

ON THE WAY

Five voices on the way

'Standing back there at the crossroads? –
I felt my life's been more like
a spaghetti junction!'

'I was in Kenya, working for Oxfam,
in Malawi working with Christian Aid, in Kurdistan …
It just feels like there's so much to do in this world,
and all I know is – I just have to do *something*.'

'So I ran round and round and worked
14-hour-days for 20 years …
Then I got cancer …
So now I'm going to concentrate more on just *being*.'

'I'm not really sure *what* my next calling is.
But I have trust
and faith.
I'll know what's right when the Spirit tells me.
I think sometimes
you just have to wait.'

'Well, it shows you God has a sense of humour anyway:
notice every time we sing –
it starts rainin' buckets!'

Neil Paynter

HIGH POINT

A grassy knoll up on the tops, on the east side of the island, heading south towards the Marble Quarry

REFLECTION

For more than thirty years the pilgrimage followed the same route – a sequence which always reached its climax at the top of Dun I. There we would look out on the islands all around us, as if we had conquered the world. And there, at the island's highest point, we would reflect on Bible stories that warned of the danger of glorying in high places. The story of the Temptations, where Jesus was led up a high mountain to look down on the nations of the world, and offered power over them. Or the story of the Transfiguration, where three disciples saw Jesus in a completely different light, and Peter wanted to hold on to that vision for ever. There at the top of Dun I we were warned of the danger of high places going to our heads, and told that like Jesus and his disciples we had to come down again: down to earth, back into the real world. And we would wind our way down Dun I and finish our journey in the graveyard chapel.

But in the year 2000 we found ourselves having to make changes to both the first and second half of the pilgrimage. Some footpaths were becoming badly eroded, and we were asked to find alternative routes. It felt like sacrilege, the very idea of changing this sacred journey. Most shocking, perhaps, was the thought of losing that final gruelling ascent of Dun I. But we were also apprehensive about the morning – losing the southward route that folk had come to know and love and replacing it with something less defined and interesting.

We need not have worried about that. Climbing over the tops on the east side of the island rather than the west gave us glimpses of a coastline we had not seen before. In fact islanders told us our new route was actually the original one! What's more, it started us thinking about other forms of pilgrimage, for people who couldn't manage this one.

And one delightful surprise: Just when we lost Dun I, we found another high point! Here! Here we look down on the tip of the Ross of Mull, and Erraid and the Paps of Jura, and out to the horizon with Colonsay and Islay … This view was opened up to us quite unexpectedly.

But what of the message we used to convey – coming to the high point only at the end of the day, to be lifted up just long enough to see the glory before descending again into real life below as the pilgrimage ends? What about this theology of worship and work, peace and politics – that we come away to beautiful places only in order to hurry back into the reality of work and pain and struggle, before we start enjoying being out of it and away from it all?

Well, here we have a different emphasis, a different way of making our journey. Instead of having our mountaintop experience near the end we have it near the beginning. Which means we won't be immediately walking away from it. Instead, as we continue round the island, reflecting on our journey through life, the high point will come with us. The emphasis is not on coming down. The emphasis is on lifting up. For today, at least, we give ourselves permission to see everything in a new light, to see glory everywhere, and to enjoy the miracle of this beautiful island, our beautiful lives and the world as it is meant to be.

Brian Woodcock, former Iona Abbey Warden

BIBLE READINGS

When all things began, the Word already was. The Word dwelt with God, and what God was, the Word was. The Word, then, was with God at the beginning, and through him all things came to be; no single thing was created without him. All that came to be was alive with his life.

John 1:1–4a (NEB)

Psalm 148
Matthew 28:16–20

PRAYER

It's different up here, God.
Different air.
Different view.
We have risen above the things that hem us in
and hold us down.
Up here, everything is lighter.
We are lighter!
We seem closer to the sky.
To heaven.
To *you*, God!
It's easier to get glimpses of glory up here;
to see why you are so pleased with everything you made –
everything alive with your life
and vibrant with light energy.

So, as we travel on, God,
closer to the sky, to heaven,
will you be coming with us?
Will you go on giving us glimpses of glory?
And will you go with us into the valleys?
And be with us to the ends of the earth?

No need to answer these questions, God.
It's enough for us to notice the difference,
to savour the moment,
and cherish today.
Tomorrow can take care of itself.
But forgive us if, as we travel together,
we occasionally wonder whether things will go *on* being different.
And whether, in fact, the difference is in *us*.
Amen

Brian Woodcock

SONGS

Glory and gratitude and praise (*Iona Abbey Music Book*, WGP)
Jesu tawa pano (*Many and Great*, Wild Goose Publications)

ON THE WAY

Pilgrims

We walk in the rain
sunshine and wind
Hair restricted under hats
            or
snapping wildly

We smile
We laugh
We walk …

An Iona pilgrim

LOST

It is an alarming experience to lose your way when you are leading a pilgrimage. You are suddenly very aware of this great line of trusting people following you, and wondering what you are going to say to them. It has happened to me two or three times, always on the way to the Marble Quarry by a new route I hadn't quite worked out yet. But only once was I completely stumped, quite unable to find the quarry at all. The worst moment of the occasion was as we all stood there in a hollow on the moorland tops, awaiting the return of Anja, our back-marker, who had gone gambolling off across the hills in search of some recognisable landmark, and it started to rain. I realised this was a good time for some appropriate reflection. I can't remember exactly what I said, but if it ended with a prayer it was probably something like this:

> God of Moses and the children of Israel,
> we may not know where we are,
> but you know,
> for no one is lost to you.

> In this unexpected pause that you give us on our journey, then,
> help us to learn what you are teaching us:

> That life is not always as clear and straightforward as we would like it to be;
> that we do not know all the answers and are not always right,
> and it does nothing for us or the gospel or you
> when we pretend otherwise;
> that life is mystery, and can never be fully known
> even by those who are trying to lead the way;
> that faith flourishes more amid honest doubt than in certainty,
> and we learn more from our failures than our successes,
> and your truth is shared most effectively
> when we listen to other people and learn from them
> and seek the way together.

But teach us, God,
that actually we *do* know where we are.
We are *here*.
Teach us to value the here and now,
because this is all we ever have,
this is what is most real,
and this, this here and now,
is our starting point.

Take us, then, one step at a time,
the way *you* want to go.

And, if it pleases you,
God of Moses and the children of Israel,
please don't leave us wandering around here for forty years
before leading us out of the wilderness!

Brian Woodcock, former Iona Abbey Warden

MARBLE QUARRY

Here at the Marble Quarry, you can see not only vast chunks of the white, green-veined marble that Iona is famous for, but also the remains of the quarrying machinery, lying abandoned since its last use in 1915. Here lie the remains of a producer gas engine, a cutting frame, a gunpowder store, and a roughly built quay, which provided the only means of transporting equipment and marble to and from the quarry.

The first written record of quarrying here dates from 1693, but it is believed that the site was worked from an earlier date than this. Apparently the original Benedictine altar was made from this marble, but was later chipped away by tourists for souvenirs. Local folklore held that a piece of Iona marble would protect the bearer from drowning, so it is perhaps not surprising that people wanted their own talismans. Even today, there are a multitude of tourist goodies made from Iona stone – and one wonders how much of Iona is scattered around the world in the form of souvenir pebbles! Larger blocks of this marble are also well travelled and have been used in monuments worldwide, for example, in the statue of Queen Victoria outside Buckingham Palace and in the Scots Kirk in Jerusalem.

The scarred rock and rusting machinery stand in stark contrast to the surrounding natural environment, and while it is tempting to interpret this as the wastefulness and desecration of industrialisation, the machinery has its own strange beauty. It is now preserved by the National Trust, and is a Scheduled Ancient Monument in its own right. However, it provides a vivid example that may help us reflect on our own relationship with the natural world, and our care of resources.

It was here that George MacLeod used to reflect on the ancient age of the rock, the expanse of history, and the limitlessness of time … How infinitesimally short our own lives seem in comparison, and yet we are wreaking enormous changes on this planet which is our home. These rocks will still be here once the machinery has long rusted away, just as the planet will survive the current changes we are inflicting on it – the question is – will we?

BIBLE READINGS

Lord, you set the mountains in place
by your strength.
You calm the roar of the seas
and the noise of the waves.
The whole world stands in awe of your deeds,
of the great things you have done.
Your deeds bring shouts of joy
from one end of the earth to another.
And every hillside
declares your glory.

Psalm 65 (adapted)

Psalm 8
Psalm 40:1–3

REFLECTION

Marble Quarry

Your marks are here –
elemental
massive
incomprehensibly long in the making.

And ours too …
ingenious,
persistent,
but so young and slight.

And I?
I am so small a thing
in this ancient cosmos
yet am known and loved by you:
my name is engraved on your palm,
your love is inscribed on my life …

and through that bearing
of one another's marks
perhaps we have both been changed …

Pat Bennett

SONGS

Christ the worker, *Free to Serve* (Hope Publishing)
From creation's start, *Iona Abbey Music Book* (Wild Goose Publications)

COLUMBA'S BAY

Columba and his followers are said to have landed on this pebbly, windswept beach in the year 563, having travelled from Ireland in a leather-bound boat known as a curragh. *Legend has it that Columba climbed to the top of a nearby hill (known as the 'Hill of the Back to Ireland') to check that his native land could no longer be seen, and thus chose Iona as the place from which to begin his missionary work. There are many tales surrounding his departure from Ireland – that it was penance for his involvement in clan battles, or for making an illicit copy of the Book of Psalms – however, these stories may be of medieval origin. In the account of Columba's life written a century after his death by Abbot Adomnán, it simply states that Columba sailed from Ireland to Britain, choosing the life of a pilgrim.*

Whatever it was that led him here, it was certainly a new beginning, and led to Iona becoming a highly influential force in the early Church, and one that reverberates to the present day. We pilgrims would not be here otherwise!

The bay is also one of the best places to find small, green pieces of Iona marble, known as 'Columba's tears'. Martin Martin, a 17th-century visitor to the island (with a somewhat tenuous grasp of geology) remarked:

'There are many pretty variegated stones on the shore below the dock; they ripen to a green colour, and are then proper for carving. The natives say these stones are fortunate, but only for some particular thing, which the person thinks fit to name, in exclusion of everything else.'

If you're hunting for these – beware of an impostor; another very attractive, greenish stone called epidote. How to tell the difference? The marble will be more translucent.

Looking around the bay, you will see several large mounds of beach stones. Popular folklore holds that these cairns were made by monks who were sent here to do penance – and some are very large mounds indeed!

Today, we use stones in our own way to reflect. It is at this stage in the pilgrimage, when we are at the furthest point away from the Abbey, that we remember Columba's journey away from the safety of the known, and consider the turning points in our own lives, before heading homeward. We remember the things that we feel may hold us back from making a fresh start, or that weigh us down as we try to journey onward. Here, we pick up two stones. One symbolic of that which we would wish to let go of – something we need to leave behind. We cast this rock into the sea, and turn, and without looking back, pick up a second stone as a sign of a new direction or commitment that we move towards, as we begin our return journey.

BIBLE READINGS

When they had brought their boats to shore, they left everything and followed him.

Luke 5:11 (NRSV)

Luke 11:9–10
1 Peter 2:4–7

REFLECTION

Going over

You have burned your bridges.

You have passed through the gate marked 'no return'
and for you, there is no going back.
No going back to the security of the known, familiar house,
to the well-worn dispensations and threadbare coverings.

Now you are out there in uncharted territory,
heavy with threat and shadows not yet entered.
The risks are high, yet you strike out boldly,
guided only by unwavering conviction
and the longing for the true centre of the land.
This is what it means to do a new thing.

And yet, you travel lightly.
You are abandoned, given up in all things
to the task that lies ahead.
Therefore, you may be exactly who you are.
You have inhabited yourself,

you are at home,
and home is where you are,
even if it is the desert.
No one can dispossess you of your own in-dwelling.
This is what it means to be free.

We stand, one foot upon the bridge,
wondering if we too have the courage to go over
and strike the match behind us.

Kathy Galloway

PRAYER

God of new beginnings

God of new beginnings,
help us to let go
and to turn our backs
on the things that hold us back,
and to hold on
to those things
that remind us of your love,
and help us to follow in your way.
Amen

Author unknown

SONGS

Behold, I make all things new (*Come All You People*, Wild Goose Publications)
Iona Gloria (*Iona Abbey Music Book*, WGP)

ON THE WAY

A sandwich blessing

Bless these sandwiches, God.
I know I made them yesterday.
I know they've been sat on.
I know, like me, they're tired
and looking a bit crumbled and worn.
But bless these sandwiches, God,
and bless me too,
and keep me travelling hopefully on.

Ruth Burgess

LOCH STAONAIG

In pre-Christian Celtic culture, lochs and rivers were dwelling places of gods, and entrances to the Otherworld. Wells and springs were sacred, and their waters had healing properties. In Christian understanding, Jesus is the water of life – the Living Water; and in baptism we are submerged, washed clean – then rise to new life …

This loch supplied the island with all its water until the early 1990s, when an EEC regulation declared it unsuitable, and a pipeline was built to bring water from Mull.

Consider how we in the Western world take the preciousness and supply of water for granted, and how seldom we think of those who, every day, must travel the distance of this pilgrimage – or much further – to collect a container of dirty water, and then carry it all the way back to their family …

BIBLE READINGS

John 7:37–38
1 Corinthians 12:13

The Samaritan woman

They came from different regions.
As different as Scotland and England.
They came from different religions
with the same roots
but different customs.
Different prophets.
Different beliefs.
But they had a common need.
Water.
And they had a common love.
Truth.
'Give me a drink,' he says.
She looks.
'How is it that you, a Jew, ask a drink from me,
a woman of Samaria?'
He smiles.
'If you knew who was asking,
you would have asked him and he would have given you "living" water.'
She squints.
'You have no bucket and the well is deep.
Where do you get this "living" water?'
She challenges.
'Are you greater than Jacob who gave us this well?'
He shrugs.
'If you drink this water, you'll be thirsty again.
The water I will give will become a spring of water,
gushing up to eternal life.'
She's no fool.
She's tired of drawing water in the heat of the day.
'Give me this water so I won't have to draw water every day.'
He points.

'Go, call your husband and come back.'
She swallows.
'I have no husband.'
He nods.
'You're right. You have had five husbands.
But the man you're living with now is not your husband.
What you have said is true.'
She stares.
How could he know that?
'You're a prophet,'
she insists.
'So … tell me who's right? Jews or Samaritans?
We Samaritans worship right here, on this mountain.
You Jews, you say Jerusalem is the place.
Who is right?'
He stares back.
'God is spirit
and those who worship must worship in spirit and in truth.'
She thinks,
What kind of an answer is that?
She declares,
'When the Messiah comes, he will tell us the truth.'
He nods.
She has given him her truth.
He offers her his truth.
'I am he.
The Messiah is talking to you.'
Hidden truth comes to light when we come face to face with God.
and when we come face to face with ourselves.
We need God,
we need truth,
as much as we need water.
In God,

in truth,
we find life.
Sometimes truth, like life, is painful.
But the living water of God's grace cleanses our pain
and renews us to go on.

God,
reveal to us the truth by which we can live with purpose
and without shame in your world.
Give us courage when we must face painful truth about ourselves.
Make us gentle when we must reveal awkward truth to others.
Cleanse us and renew us by the waters of the earth
and the living water of your love that we taste in friendship and in faith
day by day. Amen

Nancy Cocks

REFLECTIONS

Meditation

… Imagine that you are an African woman, a single mother with five children. There is no water supply in your village, and you have nearly two miles to walk to the nearest borehole to draw water. You must bring home enough to supply all your family's needs: water for drinking, cooking, for six people to have a wash, to wash all your clothes, clean the house and water your small *shamba*, a garden where you grow what food you can. You have a few chickens, and they can't survive without water either. You have to carry this water in a large metal container on your back. It weighs at least 40 kilos, and is held by a band hooked to your forehead.

On the way to work each day you also collect firewood for cooking and to keep you and the family warm when the night is cold. This too you carry on your back, on top of the metal container. You still have a baby and carry her as well … life is hard, and the water is precious.

Maureen Edwards

Water is life

Water, water everywhere! The opposite to my home country. The pilgrimage leader asked me at Loch Staonaig if I would say something to the gathering about the water situation in the country which I came from and was returning to, Uganda.

As we stood on a small island near a clean-water loch which had supplied Iona for years with fresh water, I was pleased to share something of the contrasts between home and Iona: Uganda is a landlocked country. Mains-piped water is only available in the major urban areas. 80% of the population of Uganda live in rural areas which lack adequate water supplies for domestic, animal and plant use. People have to collect water from wells, springs, boreholes or rivers. Some of these sources have been used by both animals and humans, creating a hygiene problem. In the end, this causes waterborne diseases like diarrhoea, bilharzia, typhoid and cholera.

Long distances are often walked to access the water sources. Water collection is mainly done by small children and women using containers. A lot of time is spent at water points due to large numbers of people waiting their turn. There are no big water storage tanks in rural areas, hence water has to be used sparingly, which is a huge problem in the dry season. Shortage of water has created the existence of a nomadic group of cattle-keepers commonly known as *Balaalo*. The nomads move with large herds of cattle in search of water and pasture, disrupting the traffic on roads, destroying people's gardens. Land conflict between cattle-keepers and farmers has become rampant due to water shortage. Crops die or wither away during the dry season. We rarely have irrigation facilities.

Crops can be grown during rainy season only. There is a big problem with global warming: the dry season has become longer, creating famine.

Water is life, no matter which angle one views it from; and the memories of that day at Loch Staonaig remain with me as I continue my life in Uganda, longing to return to Iona one day, if it is God's will.

Patrick Obiga, volunteer on Iona, 1999

PRAYERS

The water of life

Generous God,
forgive us that we turn the tap and forget
how precious is this gift of water.
Forgive our waste.
Forgive the little we have done to provide clean water for all.

We pray for those who must continue to walk several miles to draw water;
for those whose land is dry – who pray for rain and it does not come –
whose crops, livestock and children die;
for communities where water is contaminated and carries disease;
for people threatened by rising sea levels or flood waters.

Loving God,
as we rejoice with villages where clean water can now be drawn,
strengthen our resolve to care for all you have created,
that we may be worthy of the water of life,
that you have so lavishly given us in Jesus Christ.
Amen

Maureen Edwards

Showered with radiance

Lady Wisdom,
shower us with
your radiance;
enlightening, reflective.
Pour your waters
over our souls;
cleansing, reviving.
Baptise our dreams:
make them holy.
Wash away soul dirt,
as we cherish
your gift of water.

Chris Polhill

SONGS

Mungu ni mwema (*One Is the Body*, Wild Goose Publications)
Wash me in the water (*We Walk His Way*, WGP)

MACHAIR

'Machair' is a Gaelic term meaning 'raised beach', and it is a habitat fairly unique to the Western Isles, comprised of extremely fertile grassland. Its fertility is due in part to the seashell content of the sand which gets blown up on to the land, neutralising the acidity of the soil. Because of this, the Machair has been cultivated since Columban times. It was, and is, common land, and you can still see the impressions of the rigs used for growing crops. These plots were regularly re-allocated to ensure fair access to the most fertile areas.

Nowadays, this area is known as the 'West end common grazing', and it is still very much a shared resource, used by crofters and holidaymakers. It is even host to Iona's hotly contested annual golf tournament. More usually, golfers have to negotiate with the sheep!

So it is here that we pause to remember the gift of community, of land, and of shared resources. It is a fitting place to remember that, no matter how technologically advanced we have become since the first crops were grown on the Machair, we are still utterly dependent on the earth for our survival. We pray that we may learn to share the earth's resources more equally with our neighbours, and with generations to come.

BIBLE READINGS

Now the whole group of those who believed were of one heart and soul, and no one claimed private ownership of any possessions, but everything they owned was held in common. With great power the apostles gave their testimony to the resurrection of the Lord Jesus, and great grace was upon them all. There was not a needy person among them, for as many as owned lands or houses sold them and brought the proceeds of what was sold. They laid it at the apostles' feet, and it was distributed to each as any had need.

Acts 4:32–35 (NRSV)

John 6:26–35
Acts 2:44–47

PRAYERS

Empower me
to be a bold participant,
rather than a timid saint in waiting,
in the difficult ordinariness of now;
to exercise the authority of honesty,
rather than defer to power,
or deceive to get it;
to influence someone for justice,
rather than impress anyone for gain;
and, by grace, to find treasures
of joy, of friendship, of peace
hidden in the fields of the daily
you give me to plough.

Ted Loder

Lord of the land

Lord of the land,
it is so easy for us to reach out
and take what we want from the world.
Help us to see
when our bargain
is someone else's impoverishment;
when our pleasure is paid for
by someone else's pain.
And break our hearts
as yours is broken.

Pat Bennett

SONGS

Let's walk together (Sarantañani) (*Sent by the Lord*, WGP)
Silently we look with God (*We Walk His Way*, Wild Goose Publications)

TEA BREAK

The Machair is also where the on- and off-road pilgrimages come together to share tea and flapjack. In honour of this much-valued tradition – especially on a cold, wet day – here's the recipe:

Flapjack (makes 24)

INGREDIENTS
(use fairtrade where possible):

❖ *500g porridge oats*

❖ *170g coconut*

❖ *340g margarine*

❖ *170g sugar*

❖ *250g golden syrup*

❖ *250g treacle*

❖ *1 teaspoon salt*

1. Preheat the oven to gas mark 4, 350°F/180°C.

2. Melt sugar, treacle, syrup and margarine over a low heat.

3. Stir in the porridge oats, coconut and salt and mix well.

4. Press the mixture into a baking tin to approximately 2cm thick.

5. Bake in the oven until the mixture begins to harden at the edges, but the centre is still soft: about 20 minutes.

6. Leave to cool slightly, then mark into squares with a knife.

7. When cool enough to handle, turn out the squares to cool on a wire tray.

8. Serve from the back of a van – come rain or shine.

A grace

O God,
to those who have hunger give bread,
to us who have bread
give hunger for justice.

From South America

HILL OF THE ANGELS

This enigmatic-looking hummock has two names, both relating to the supposed power of the place. One name, 'Cnoc nan Aingeal', means 'Hill of the Angels', and is linked to Saint Columba through the following tale, as told by his biographer, Adomnán, about a century after Columba's death:

'Likewise, on another occasion, when St Columba was living in Iona, he addressed the assembled brethren, making his point with great emphasis, saying:

"Today I shall go to the machair on the west coast of our island, and I wish to go alone. No one is to follow me therefore."

They obeyed and he set out alone as he desired. But one of the brethren, who was an artful scout, took a different route and hid himself on the top of a little hill that overlooks the machair, for he was eager to find out why the saint had gone out alone. From his vantage point, he could see St Columba standing on a knoll among the fields and praying with his arms spread out towards heaven and his eyes gazing upwards. Strange to tell – look! – there was suddenly a marvellous apparition, which the man could see with his own bodily eyes from his position on that nearby hill …

For holy angels, the citizens of the heavenly kingdom, were flying down with amazing speed, dressed in white robes, and began to gather around the holy man as he prayed. After they had conversed a little with St Columba, the heavenly crowd – as though they could feel that they were being spied on– quickly returned to the heights of heaven.

St Columba himself, after this conference with angels, went back to the monastery, where he again called the brethren together. He reproached them severely and asked which of them was guilty of disobedience. They protested that they did not know what he referred to, but the man, who was aware of his own inexcusable disobedience, could not bear to hide his sin any longer. He knelt in front of St Columba in the sight of all the brethren and begged his forgiveness. The Saint took the brother aside, laying stern threats on him, as he knelt, and charged him never to give away to anyone the least part of the secret concerning his angelic vision so long as the Saint should live.'

... This seems to have happened – but then:

'After St Columba had left the body, the man disclosed to the brethren how he had seen the apparition of the heavenly host, and publicly affirmed what he said. Hence today the knoll where St Columba conferred with angels affirms by its very name what took place there, for it is called Cnoc nan Aingeal, that is, the angels' knoll' (from Adomnán's *Life of St Columba*).

Now, as well as being Columba's biographer, Adomnán, who was Abbot of Iona, was also the author and chief promulgator of the Law of the Innocents. *This was described as 'the first law in heaven and earth for the protection of women', but was also intended to protect other non-combatants, such as children and clergy. As such, it has been interpreted as a precursor of the Geneva Convention and the UN Declaration on Human Rights; and it finds a link in the present-day work of the Iona Community, with its commitment to non-violence and action for justice and peace.*

The other name for this place is 'Sithean Mor', or 'Fairy Mound', possibly dating from pre-Christian times. There are tales of local customs involving fires being lit on the hill (the Gaelic word aingeal *can mean both 'angel' and 'fire'), and cattle being driven through them for purification as part of the May festival of Beltane.*

It is easy to see how myths and legends can become appropriated in our search for meaning – holy places for an earlier community becoming adopted into a newer world-view. Today, the tales of Columba and the 'Celtic church' are often reinterpreted as parables for our own contemporary concerns – often a yearning for a simpler, more connected life. However, we should perhaps tread carefully on the boundary between finding inspiration in these stories – or merely appropriating them as a form of escapism into a pleasant, privatised piety. Columba did not seek a retreat, but travelled on a mission.

BIBLE READINGS

Jacob was left alone; and a man wrestled with him until daybreak. When the man saw that he did not prevail against Jacob, he struck him on the hip socket; and Jacob's hip was put out of joint as he wrestled with him. Then he said, 'Let me go, for the day is breaking.' But Jacob said, 'I will not let you go, unless you bless me.' So he said to him, 'What is your name?' And he said, 'Jacob.' Then the man said, 'You shall no longer be called Jacob, but Israel, for you have striven with God and with humans, and have prevailed.' Then Jacob asked him, 'Please tell me your name?' But he said, 'Why is it that you ask my name?' And there he blessed him. So Jacob called the place Peniel, saying, 'For I have seen God face to face, and yet my life is preserved.'

Genesis 32:24–30 (NRSV)

Luke 2:8–14
Acts 12:6–10

PRAYER

Ordinary, extraordinary God

We thank you, God, for the enchanting.
For the things that pluck us
out of our everyday experience –
however briefly –
and tantalise us with glimpses of mystery.

For extraordinary wonders of angels,
shooting stars, impossible coincidences,
and things that go bump in the night.

And for ordinary wonders;
such as the way a plain cheese sandwich
seems like a gourmet banquet
when carried for miles and eaten outside.

Ordinary, extraordinary God,
thank you for reminding us that the world, and you,
are bigger than we can possibly imagine.

Jane Bentley

SONGS

Alleluia (South Africa) (*Sent by the Lord*, WGP)
From Erin's shores (*Love from Below,* Wild Goose Publications)
(*This could also be read as a poem.*)

THE HERMIT'S CELL

This ring of stones is all that remains of an ancient beehive cell, or of an old shieling or enclosure. It's certainly possible that it was a monks' cell (it resembles the remains of other beehive cells on islands around Iona), and that it was later used for agricultural purposes. It's nice to think of a solitary monk out here, meditating in the peace and quiet; and of a farm girl out here, milking the cows while listening to the linnets and lapwings: work and worship cosmically intertwined.

In Columba's time, about 600 monks were living and working together on the island, and so the centre of the community – like today – was far from tranquil and still. Iona itself was a crossroads of the world, the sea being the 'highway' of the day. Celtic scholar Ian Bradley writes:

… The monastic life was far from being one of retreat and escape. Indeed, monasteries were almost certainly the busiest institutions in Celtic society, constantly teeming with people and fulfilling the roles of school, library, hospital, guest house, arts centre and mission station. Most of the great Celtic saints alternated between periods of intense activity and involvement in administrative affairs with lengthy spells of quiet reflection and months spent alone in a cell on a remote island or rocky promontory. In this, they were following the example of their Lord and Saviour, one moment surrounded by crowds and engaged in preaching, teaching and healing, and the next walking alone by the lakeside or engaged in quiet prayer in the mountains. Columba's life exemplified this balanced rhythm. At times he was busily engaged in founding monasteries, negotiating with kings, attending councils, going on missionary journeys and ruling his ever expanding monastic *familia*. Yet his biographers also portray him spending long periods praying or copying Scriptures … He frequently took himself to Hinba for solitary retreats. In many ways this combination of action and meditation provided a perfect example of what modern theologians call 'praxis' – a combination of involvement in practical issues and theological reflection on them. In the words of a poem written about him just a year or two after his death, '*What he conceived keeping vigil, by action he ascertained.*'[1]

BIBLE READINGS

At that place he came to a cave, and spent the night there.

Then the word of the Lord came to him, saying, 'What are you doing here, Elijah?' He answered, 'I have been very zealous for the Lord, the God of hosts; for the Israelites have forsaken your covenant, thrown down your altars, and killed your prophets with the sword. I alone am left, and they are seeking my life, to take it away.'

He said, 'Go out and stand on the mountain before the Lord, for the Lord is about to pass by.' Now there was a great wind, so strong that it was splitting mountains and breaking rocks in pieces before the Lord, but the Lord was not in the wind; and after the wind an earthquake, but the Lord was not in the earthquake; and after the earthquake a fire, but the Lord was not in the fire; and after the fire a sound of sheer silence. When Elijah heard it, he wrapped his face in his mantle and went out and stood at the entrance of the cave …

1 Kings 19:9–13 (NRSV)

Matthew 4:1–11
Matthew 11:28–30
Mark 6:30–32

MEDITATION

Modern life feels increasingly noisy, distracting and cluttered … Life is full of conflicting messages – advertisements, government and corporate propaganda, cascades of emails, texts, phone calls … It's a world of juggle juggle: work, family, friends, relationships. It's do, do, do, with little time to *be* to feed all the doing … In our world of busyness and babble, it's so difficult to find a still centre; to hear the 'still small voice' …

Sit down on a stone or on the grass, or stand comfortably, and spend the next five minutes or so in silence, listening for God and to God, or simply being relaxed, still and quiet in a world that is *so* full of activity and noise.

A volunteer working at the centres on Iona wrote: *'I believe that all of us have a hermitage like this ring of stones inside our hearts … We can be quiet and enter into that space to meet with God.'*

(Time of silence …)

REFLECTIONS

A score of years ago, a friend placed in my hand a book called *True Peace*. It was an old mediaeval message, and it had but one thought – that God was waiting in the depths of my being to talk to me if I would only get still enough to hear His voice.

I thought this would be a very easy matter, and so began to get still. But I had no sooner commenced than a perfect pandemonium of voices reached my ears, a thousand clamouring notes from without and within, until I could hear nothing but their noise and din.

Some were my own voices, my own questions, some my very prayers. Others were suggestions of the tempter and the voices from the world's turmoil.

In every direction, I was pulled and pushed and greeted with noisy acclamations and unspeakable unrest. It seemed necessary for me to listen to some of them and to answer some of them; but God said, 'Be still, and know that I am God.' Then came the conflict of thoughts for tomorrow, and its duties and cares; but God said, 'Be still.'

And as I listened, and slowly learned to obey, and shut my ears to every sound, I found after a while that when the other voices ceased, or I ceased to hear them, there was a still small voice in the depths of my being that began to speak with an inexpressible tenderness, power and comfort …

A.B. Simpson

Hermit's Cell paradox

How can a place engender
such quietness
… and yet be so full of music?

How can a place hold
such stillness
… and yet release such energy?

How can a place be
so small
… and yet encompass the cosmos?

How can a place exist
in time
… but open into eternity?

This is a place
of deep paradox;

but such
is the language of God,
    who was both human
        … and divine.

Pat Bennett

PRAYERS

Now, O Lord,
calm me into a quietness that heals and listens,
that moulds my longings and passions,
my wounds and wonderings
into a more holy, human shape.
In the silence let me listen
and hear the truth you have put into me;
trust the love you have for me
which you call me to live out
with all my sisters and brothers in your human family.

Ted Loder

At the Hermit's Cell

Lord of the silences –
speak to me:
in the blowing of the wind;
in the rustling of the grass;
in the sound of the sea;
in the beating of my heart;

in the stirring of my spirit –
speak, Lord.
I am listening.

Pat Bennett

Blessing

Deep peace of the running wave to you
Deep peace of the flowing air to you
Deep peace of the quiet earth to you
Deep peace of the shining stars to you
Deep peace of the Son of Peace to you

A Celtic blessing

SONGS

Be still and know (*There Is One Among Us*, Wild Goose Publications)
Bless the Lord, my soul (Taizé)

MEDITATION ON A STILE

A reflection for when the pilgrimage arrives at the stile, on the way back from the Hermit's Cell. (Brian Woodcock, former Abbey Warden, used to deliver this reflection while sitting on top of the stile – hence the title.)

When we were asked to change the route of the pilgrimage at the north end of the island, and stop taking it over Dun I, Jan Sutch Pickard (Deputy Warden) and I explored various ways back from the Hermit's Cell to the road.

Always we found ourselves crossing people's land, sinking into mud or barred by boundary walls and fences. That was so for this route as much as any other. In fact at this particular point we met all the obstacles at once!

But as we know, every problem is an opportunity. The people whose land we are on agreed not only that we could cross it but also that we could put stepping stones across the mud and a stile over the fence. The stile was built by volunteers working for the Scottish National Trust. And the stepping stones?

Well, the difficulty with the stones was that there just weren't any lying around here. But we had plenty of good big ones back at the MacLeod Centre. Jan and I carried a few to this spot and laid them carefully in what during the winter was a small stream. They sank into the mud and disappeared from view. I volunteered to bring some more here the next day.

So next day I went prepared. I took my rucksack to 'the Mac' so I could take more. I only expected to put a few large stones in the bag, but discovered that once it was on my back it seemed quite light. So I put some more in. In fact I filled it up. My load was still quite manageable. So off I went with it.

Unfortunately, however, I lost my way. I wandered back and forth, expecting to find the wall and muddy stream any moment. But the first place I recognised was the Hermit's Cell. I couldn't believe I had gone so far out of my way!

From the Hermit's Cell I could easily trace my way to the muddy stream, for I was now going in the direction of our new pilgrimage route. But by now the load on my back had become almost impossibly heavy. That last stretch from the Hermit's Cell to here was sheer agony!

But at least, as I piled my stones into the stream, they didn't all sink from view. And as I slowly straightened my back before limping back to the Abbey I had the satisfaction of being able to admire what just about passed as stepping stones. So I plead with you not to take them for granted. Think of the blood, sweat and tears that went into placing them here so that you could cross safely. Ah! – I know you are more likely to remember the foolishness of someone who over-filled his bag and then got himself lost. Well, perhaps that's the lot of those whose calling is to serve! I jest of course. But it's not such a bad thing to be a fool for Christ.

For me this place is all about crossing barriers and boundaries. Boundaries are necessary. But there are some controversial ones in the world today that need challenging. We think now of the Israelis and Palestinians. We used to think of Berlin. And Belfast. And South Africa. Walls of separation, some physical, all apparently impenetrable.

They called the one in West Belfast the Peace Line. It was built to keep two areas apart: the Falls and the Shankill. But there on the Peace Line, on the Springfield Road, a small community sprung up during the Troubles, bringing Catholics and Protestants together to pray, talk and share their lives. It was called The Cornerstone Community. And further up the Peace Line an urban farm was created, inviting children and young people from both sides of the divide to care for the animals. The high wire fence formed the boundary of one side of the farm; but then they bought a field on the other side of it, and put a goat in it. And so that volunteers could feed and care for the goat they cut a hole in the fence and made a gate for them to go through. Just to look after the goat, you understand!

For me, stepping stones and stiles are not just about crossing rough ground. They are reminders of a role we are invited to play in our divided world. A prophetic, even subversive, role. One of challenging inhuman walls of separation with bridges and gateways, dialogue and relationships. Finding ways through. Finding better ways of living together in our world.

Brian Woodcock

DUN I

Dun I, which simply means 'Hill of Iona', is the highest spot on the island (332 feet above sea level). On a clear day, the view is glorious – to the north are the Treshnish Isles (including the Dutchman's Cap) and Staffa, and in the far distance, the Cuillins of Skye; to the south, the Paps of Jura; to the west, the lighthouse of Skerryvore off Tiree; and to the east, Ben More, the highest mountain on Mull, appearing over the back of the Berg, with its striated basalt cliffs. Lying just off Mull's coast are the islands of Gometra and Ulva. And down below, is the south end of Iona, and the Machair, and the way you have just walked.

Coming to Iona can offer people the chance to see their life journey from a different perspective; to stand back and take stock …

Take a moment now to appreciate the view … To wonder at the glory and power of God's creation … To feel the elements, and remember that you are alive …

From up here, you might gaze around at the infinite sky and ocean, and think about how small you are in the scheme of things. And yet the wonder is that God cares for each one of us. We are all precious in God's sight (Isaiah 43:4). God formed us in the womb (Psalm 139) – even the very hairs on our head are numbered (Matthew 10:30) …

For some, Iona is a place of epiphanies or of spiritual highs. 'Heightened moments'. 'Hilltop experiences'. Yet we can't remain above it all. We have to come back down to the earth again: the disciples who witnessed the Transfiguration on the mountaintop went on to Jerusalem, to Jesus Christ's crucifixion, death, and resurrection. From this beautiful, seemingly removed spot, the White Strand of the Monks at the north-eastern tip of the island may be picked out, where, in the 9th century, the Abbot and fifteen monks were slaughtered by marauding Vikings: an ancient story with parallels to many news reports today, in the 21st century …

God, we pray that we may never retreat or seek to extract ourselves from the everyday suffering and grassroots struggles of the oppressed and marginalised people of the earth. Help us to use your energy and vision to fight and challenge the Powers of the world that keep your people down.

BIBLE READINGS

Six days later, Jesus took with him Peter and James and John, and led them up a high mountain apart, by themselves. And he was transfigured before them, and his clothes became dazzling white, such as no one on earth could bleach them. And there appeared to them Elijah with Moses, who were talking with Jesus. Then Peter said to Jesus, 'Rabbi, it is good for us to be here; let us make three dwellings, one for you, one for Moses, and one for Elijah.' He did not know what to say, for they were terrified. Then a cloud overshadowed them, and from the cloud there came a voice, 'This is my Son, the Beloved; listen to him!' Suddenly when they looked around, they saw no one with them any more, but only Jesus.

Mark 9:2–8 (NRSV)

Psalm 121
Matthew 2:1–12

REFLECTIONS

When

When I ascend to the mountaintop
and gaze with joy on the other side,
or when I must travel to places of death;
cherish my delight, and contain my horror,
for you have been there, and there, before me,
O Jesus of the Way.

And when my journey takes me far across the world
and I must encounter new tongues, new ideas, new ways,

hold my heart and mind open,
for you are there too, waiting to welcome me,
O Jesus of the Way.

And when my path is black and unlit,
and I can see nothing in front but dark and fearful shapes,
still my panic enough to know
that one of them is your shape,
O Jesus of the Way

For where shall I go from your spirit,
and how could I be away from your presence?

If I climb up to the heavens, you are there,
and if I make my bed in hell, still you are there.

If I fly east with the rising sun,
or sail to the uttermost west, you are there.

If darkness covers me, and night closes in on me,
you are there too;
for night is not dark for you, but luminous as the day,
and the two are one to you.

For where shall I go from your spirit?
You presence is there, and there, and there.

Kathy Galloway

At least once in your life …

Take a crazy diversion
Visit the top of a mountain
Be storm-swept by wind and rain
Sleep under the stars

Sing
Smell the blossom as spring arrives
Open your mouth and catch raindrops
Lie down and watch

     satellites cross space

Stand under a tree and look up
In a rock pool and look down
Sit by a beach-fire till it burns to embers
Spend time in your own company
Listen to the sound of waves through a window

Discover love
Discover silence

Fiona Caley

PRAYERS

Glimpses of glory

Lord, you offer us glimpses of your glory
in the world you have made –
through worship and prayer,
through other people.

But we confess, Lord, that, like the early disciples,
we do not know how to react.
We love the glimpses of your glory.
We long for spiritual 'highs'.
We would live with you on the mountaintop of faith,
for we do not know how to reflect your glory
in our everyday lives on the plains.

Lord, forgive us for rarely allowing you to transfigure our lives
with the glory of your love.
Fill us with the light of your Spirit,
that, in all our dealings with other people,
in all that we think and do and say,
your glory may be revealed.

Author unknown

On Dun I

Lord of the high places –
fill me with your power:
– creating power of the Father;
– life-giving power of the Son;
– liberating power of the Spirit.

May I know such an infilling of You
that my life may be no longer silent,
but become a glorious, joyful affirmation
of your kingdom.

Pat Bennett

SONGS

Behold, I make all things new (*Come All You People*, WGP)
Gloria (Argentina) (*Many and Great*, Wild Goose Publications)

REILIG ODHRÁIN/ST ORAN'S CHAPEL

This is the oldest remaining building on the island, dating back to the 12th century, however, the surrounding burial ground has probably been in continuous use since Columban times, and it remains the burial ground for islanders today. Iona has a long tradition of being an especially holy place for burial – a 16th-century source asserts that there are 48 Scottish, 8 Norwegian and 4 Irish kings buried here. Among these are the legendary Duncan and Macbeth, of Shakespearean fame. However, this tradition may be older still: close by lie the remains of a 4000-year-old Bronze Age burial cairn, evidence, perhaps, that Iona had pre-Christian significance as a final resting place.

There is a grisly (but presumably apocryphal) burial legend associated with the chapel: that, in order to consecrate the chapel, a willing sacrifice needed to be offered in the form of a monk being buried alive, and that Oran (after whom the chapel is named) gamely volunteered himself for the task. Apparently, three days after his burial, Columba opened the grave to gaze once more upon his brother – to find Oran still conscious, saying: 'There is no such great wonder in death, nor is Hell what it has been described …' Oran was quickly buried again, before he could reveal anything further.

And echoes of this legend can still be found today, where church institutions suppress questions or debate, or cover up institutional abuse to preserve authority and public image. Our all-too-human failings at times obscure the transformational teaching of Jesus – but 'the light that shines in the darkness' will always prevail.

We end our pilgrimage in a graveyard, remembering that that is where the Resurrection faith began.

BIBLE READINGS

On the first day of the week, at early dawn, they came to the tomb, taking the spices that they had prepared. They found the stone rolled away from the tomb, but when they went in, they did not find the body. While they were perplexed about this, suddenly two men in dazzling clothes stood beside them. The women were terrified and bowed their faces to the ground, but the men said to them, 'Why do you look for the living among the dead? He is not here, but has risen.'

Luke 24:1–6 (NRSV)

Ezekiel 37:1–14
John 11:32–43

REFLECTION

I never wanted to be born

This meditation was written originally for the funeral service of a group of teenagers who had been killed in a car crash. It should be read slowly.

> I never wanted to be born.
>
> The older I grew,
> the fonder I became
> of my mother's womb
> and its warmth
> and its safety.
>
> I feared the unknown:
>   the next world,
> about which I knew nothing
> but imagined the worst.

Yet, as I grew older,
I sensed in my soul
that the womb was not my home for ever.

Though I did not know when,
I felt sure that one day
I would disappear through a door
which had yet to be opened,
and confront the unknown
of which I was afraid.

And then,
it happened.

In blood, tears and pain,
it happened.

I was cut off from the familiar;
I left my life behind
and discovered not darkness but light,
     not hostility but love,
     not eternal separation
but hands that wanted to hold me.

(Pause)

I never wanted to be born.

I don't want to die.

The older I grow,
the fonder I become
of this world
and its warmth
and its safety.

I fear the unknown:
        the next world,
about which I know nothing
but imagine the worst.

Yet as I grow older,
I sense in my soul
that this world is not my home for ever.

Though I do not know when,
I feel that one day
I will disappear through a door
which has yet to be opened.

Perhaps having come so safely through the first door,
I should not fear so hopelessly the second.

John L. Bell

Blessing

May God's goodness be yours,
and well, and seven times well, may you spend your lives:
may you be an isle in the sea,
may you be a hill on the shore,
may you be a star in the darkness,
may you be a staff to the weak;
and may the power of the Spirit
pour on you, richly and generously,
today, and in the days to come.

Celtic blessing

SONGS

Ameni (*There Is One Among Us*, Wild Goose Publications)
Themba Amen (*We Walk His Way*, WGP)

THE ON-ROAD PILGRIMAGE

ON THE WAY

Encounter

Lord,
I ask only this:
that you would meet me
on the road;
and that I, expectant,
would recognise and know you
in your coming

and so find my life
transformed.

Pat Bennett

ST MARTIN'S CROSS (SEE PAGE 17)

DUNSMEORACH

Dunsmeorach is a Gaelic word meaning 'Hill of the Song Thrush'.

George MacLeod, Founder of the Iona Community, lived here for a period with his family. At present, members of the Iona Community's Resident Group live here, sharing the big, beautiful, old white house and life in community.

Iona is such a beautiful, poetic, seemingly ideal place to live, and the Abbey can sometimes feel so much like God's house on earth, that you wish you could stay here forever ... But George MacLeod's vision back in the 1930s, while rebuilding the Abbey with a community of ministers and craftsmen, wasn't of people staying here forever, wasn't 'banishment to a lonely isle', or 'playing Franciscans' ... George's idea was for ministers and craftsmen to come to Iona to work together and learn from each other, and then go back to the city to help rebuild the 'common life'.

These days, Resident staff and volunteers come to Iona to work for a short period (from between two months to three years), and then go back out into the wider world, taking what they've learned and experienced on Iona into their communities. Many come back to Iona from time to time to 'get recharged' or to 'reconnect'.

Murphy Davis, a founding member of the Open Door Community in Atlanta, Georgia, a Catholic-worker-inspired community who serve the homeless, said in a sermon in Iona Abbey: 'Our hearts are set on pilgrim roads not to satisfy ourselves with finding one holy place, not to romanticise this thin place, but to take the experience of the presence of the Holy back into the thick of things ...'

Think for a moment about the community you live in. Think about finding the holy in midst of life there: grace, forgiveness, reconciliation, resurrection ... Think about taking the experience, energy and spirit of Iona back into your everyday, 'back into the thick of things' ...

BIBLE READINGS

Moses was keeping the flock of his father-in-law Jethro, the priest of Midian; he led his flock beyond the wilderness, and came to Horeb, the mountain of God. There the angel of the Lord appeared to him in a flame of fire out of a bush; he looked, and the bush was blazing, yet it was not consumed. Then Moses said, 'I must turn aside and look at this great sight, and see why the bush is not burned up.' When the Lord saw that he had turned aside to see, God called to him out of the bush, 'Moses, Moses!' And he said, 'Here I am.' Then he said, 'Come no closer! Remove the sandals from your feet, for the place on which you are standing is holy ground.' He said further, 'I am the God of your father, the God of Abraham, the God of Isaac, and the God of Jacob.' And Moses hid his face, for he was afraid to look at God.

Exodus 3:1–6 (NRSV)

Psalm 139:7–12
Luke 17:20

REFLECTIONS

Prescript

A boy threw a stone at the stained-glass window of the Incarnation. It nicked out the 'E' in the word HIGHEST in the text GLORY TO GOD IN THE HIGHEST. Thus, till unfortunately it was mended, it read, GLORY TO GOD IN THE HIGH ST.

At least the mended E might have been contrived on a swivel so that in a high wind it would have been impossible to see which way it read. Such is the genius, and the offence, of the Christian revelation. Holiness, salvation, glory are all come down to earth in Jesus Christ our Lord. Truth is found in the constant interaction of the claim that the apex of the Divine Majesty is declared in Christ's humanity.

The Word of God cannot be dissociated from the Action of God. As the blood courses through the body, so the spiritual is alone kept healthy in its interaction in the High Street. God's revelation of Himself was not a series of mighty acts done to Israel, but a series performed in and through Israel as a community in the totality of its life …

George MacLeod, from Only One Way Left

Jacob's Luz becomes his Bethel (Genesis 28)

This 'sermon' was given at an agape service at the end of a week on Iona.

He was on a sort of pilgrimage, Jacob.
A sort of 'pilgrimage through life':
a journey to an uncertain new home
in the hope of finding work and,
under pressure from his father, Isaac,
a wife.

The sort of uncertain and vulnerable pilgrimage through life
that most of us are on,
most of the time.

And he found himself in a very ordinary place, Jacob:
a shelter for the night on a rock in a town called Luz.

The sort of place you just pitch your tent, then pass on through
without really giving it a second look.

The sort of place where we all spend our lives,
most of the time.

But ordinary places can become extraordinary
if the eyes of our hearts are opened to see them that way.

And ordinary journeys through life can be transformed wondrously,
anywhere,
by encounters with the Divine.

So in the dark of a dreary night
on a campsite in humdrum Luz
the seeker Jacob met God in a dream,

and God promised him a certain future;
a blessed future;
a future full of promises which far exceeded any aims and intentions
that young man had;
a future which only his father Isaac might have imagined
or hoped for his son.

As Jacob woke up from this life-transforming dream
the eyes of his heart were opened
to see the place he was in
in a very new way.

'Surely God is in this place – and I did not know it!' he said, amazed.
'This is an awesome place,' he said, astonished. 'Surely it is the House
of God – it's a gate that leads to heaven!'

And he renamed Luz, Bethel, which means 'House of God'.

And Bethel has ever since been known as a holy place
to many religious traditions
and many hopeful travellers-through-life ...

We find ourselves together here today
in a place which has long been thought of as holy
(though a place of hard work and honest toil – an everyday place – for
those who have made this exposed slice of rock their home).

And we offer each other peace
for our onward journeys:
maybe journeys like Jacob's –
pilgrimages through life,
hoping and dreaming.
So we celebrate today
that our Luz can become our Bethel,

if we open the eyes of our hearts
to the possibility
of the Divine breaking into our everyday lives.
And we can leave this holy place
(whether tomorrow or on another day)
in the firm faith
that any place
and every place to which we travel
can be a house we share with God
can be a gate which opens us to heaven.

John Davies

PRAYER

Outside holiness

O Christ, you are within each of us …
it is our own inner being you have renewed.
We are your temple not made with hands.
We are your body.
If every wall should crumble, and every church decay,
we are your habitation.
Nearer are you than breathing,
closer than hands and feet.
Ours are the eyes with which you, in the mystery,
look out with compassion on the world.
Yet we bless you for this place,
for your directing of us, your redeeming of us,
and your indwelling.
Take us outside, O Christ, outside holiness,
out to where soldiers curse and nations clash

at the crossroads of the world …
We ask it for your own name's sake.
Amen

George MacLeod

SONGS

Thuma mina (*Sent by the Lord*, Wild Goose Publications)
We will take what you offer (*There Is One Among Us*, WGP)

ON THE WAY

Holy ground

City streets
city centre
outskirts, edges, margins
concrete jungle
cardboard city
wasteland
urban wilderness

Remove the sandals from your feet,
for the place on which you are standing is holy ground.

Housing estate
slum
shanty town
bedsit, penthouse
dockside development, silent shipyard
high-rise, towerblock, tenement, prison
shop doorway, park bench, street corner
railway arches, under bridges, Underground stations
ghettos
(of poverty)
ghettos
(of privilege)

Remove the sandals from your feet,
for the place on which you are standing is holy ground.

Fences, walls, barbed wire
noise, din
clamour, chaos
rubbish, heat, stench
fast cars, traffic jams, exhaust fumes, gridlock
shopping malls
multiplex cinemas
parks
playgrounds
backyards
allotments
rooftop gardens
Church
Cathedral
Mosque
Gurdwara
Synagogue
Temple

Remove the sandals from your feet,
for the place on which you are standing is holy ground.

Amen

Sandra Fox (adapted)

THE PARISH CHURCH

Following the Reformation, the Benedictine abbey, the Augustinian nunnery, and St Ronan's Church (the 'parish church' on Iona since about 1200) all went into decline.* There wasn't a parish church on Iona again until 1828, when this church, designed by Thomas Telford, was constructed. It was one of the 'Parliamentary churches': churches paid for by Parliament as part of a rebuilding of the Church across the Highlands and islands during that period.

Think of your church back home. Does it feel like a church that is growing, or does it feel like a church in decline? … Are numbers important in the end? Or is the Kingdom about a quality, not quantity? … Think about what your church does well; and what it could do better. Is it a place where the stranger is welcomed; a place of acceptance and unconditional love; a place where all members' gifts are included and celebrated? …

*St Ronan's Church, which is now the Nunnery museum, was restored in the 1870s, the 1920s and the early 1990s, and now houses some of the Nunnery's early-medieval sculpted stones. Evidence of a much earlier church than St Ronan's was discovered beneath its foundations, along with traces of burials, during an archaeological dig in the 1990s. The chapel and bones may date from the early Christian period. St Ronan was an 8th-century saint.

BIBLE READINGS

Now there are varieties of gifts, but the same Spirit; and there are varieties of services, but the same Lord; and there are varieties of activities, but it is the same God who activates all of them in everyone. To each is given the manifestation of the Spirit for the common good. To one is given through the Spirit the utterance of wisdom, to another the utterance of knowledge according to the same Spirit, to another faith by the same spirit, to another gifts of healing by the one Spirit, to another the working of miracles, to another prophecy, to another the discernment of spirits, to another various kinds of tongues, to another the interpretation of tongues. All these are activated by the one and the same Spirit, who allots to each one individually just as the Spirit chooses.

1 Corinthians 12:4–11 (NRSV)

Luke 4:14–21
1 Corinthians 12:14–26
Ephesians 4:1–16

REFLECTION

God in the thick of things and beyond
(A house church at worship, Panama)

They gathered frequently to pray as a group, together with the women and with Mary the mother of Jesus and with his brothers. Acts 1:14 (GNB)

One night, when a planned engagement fell through, I wandered among the homes of the community. There I met a man, Bill, whom I had previously talked to as he was washing a car. Nine months ago he had been a hopeless drunk. Now he lived by doing odd jobs.

I asked if there was anything happening which I could attend. He said he was a lay minister and was just going to conduct a liturgy of the Word. I would be welcome to come along. He was still in the same creased shirt and trousers in which he had washed the car.

The bare house in which we met was really one room, with partitions breaking it up into a bedroom, and a bedroom/kitchen. On the kitchen table was a cross, with a lighted candle on either side. Over his open-necked shirt, Bill placed a 'yoke' or stole and was ready to start. About ten neighbours pressed in, some bringing their own chairs or stools with them. For a good part of the service, two of the children of the household were crying intermittently; occasionally one would get up to pull back the curtain and gaze at us. Outside dogs barked and howled, competing with a transistor radio. I shared with an older man a couch whose middle had the flock showing through. Most of those who took part were in their twenties or early thirties.

There was an introductory section in which people sang and gave responses. Then a passage from the Acts of the Apostles, used throughout the parish that week, was taken for study. Practically everyone participated in building up an understanding of the passage. At one point Bill seemed to be pushing them too strongly in emphasising God's presence in the midst of life. They would not have it. 'We know God is in the thick of things where we are,' they said. 'We believe that. But that is not all. God is also beyond us. We don't know how he can be with us and beyond us. But that's just the way it is.'

After about forty minutes of Bible study, those who took part were asked to offer prayers and all but two responded. Another song was sung, there were one or two more responses, and the service ended.

Ian M. Fraser

PRAYERS

Pray for:

– Christians around the world, and people of all faiths, who are persecuted for what they believe in … Pray for their safety, and that one day they may be free to worship openly …

– those imprisoned for their beliefs …

– basic Christian communities around the world … giving thanks that, amid poverty and oppression, people are finding a biblical faith that empowers and liberates, as they work together for grassroots change …[2]

– your church or community back home …

– the folk who meet here each Sunday …

Prayer

Lord God, whose Son was content to die to bring new life,
have mercy on your Church which will do anything you ask,
anything at all, except die and be reborn.

Lord Christ, forbid us unity which leaves us where we are:
welded into one company but extracted from the battle;
engaged to be yours,
but not found at your side.

Holy Spirit of God,
reach deeper than our inertia and fears:
release us into the freedom of children of God.

Ian M. Fraser

SONGS

Come now, O Prince of Peace (*Sent by the Lord*, Wild Goose Publications)
Sent by the Lord (*Sent by the Lord*, WGP)

MACLEAN'S CROSS

MacLean's Cross dates from the 15th century and is a product of the artistically significant Iona school of stone-carving. It was likely commissioned by a member of the Clan MacLean of Duart and Lochbuie, who were a powerful family in the isles at the time.

In the Middle Ages, two tracks and a street met here, so the cross marks a crossroads. On the east side of MacLean's Cross (facing you) is an interweaving Celtic pattern of plaitwork and foliage. On the west face, at the top, is a carving of Christ crucified …

BIBLE READINGS

When it was noon, darkness came over the whole land until three in the afternoon. At three o'clock Jesus cried out with a loud voice, 'Eloi, Eloi, lema sabachthani?' which means, 'My God, my God, why have you forsaken me?' When some of the bystanders heard it, they said, 'Listen, he is calling for Elijah.' And someone ran, filled a sponge with sour wine, put it on a stick, and gave it to him to drink, saying, 'Wait, let us see whether Elijah will come to take him down.' Then Jesus gave a loud cry and breathed his last. And the curtain of the temple was torn in two, from top to bottom. Now when the centurion, who stood facing him, saw that in this way he breathed his last, he said, 'Truly this man was God's Son!'

Mark 15:33–39 (NRSV)

Mark 15:21–32
John 20:19–22

PRAYERS

O Jesus, you weren't only crucified 2000 years ago.
You are being crucified today –
here and now …

We pray for those who are being crucified here and now:

We pray for those being crucified by poverty:
in Sudan, in Easterhouse in Glasgow …

For victims of capitalism and other powers;
for those struggling under the burden of unfair debt and trade,
unfair debt and trade we profit by.

We pray for children being crucified.
Children working in sweatshops around the world.
Children who make the clothes we wear,
who help to harvest
the food we eat.

We pray for women being crucified.
Women working in the sex trade in London, in Bangkok …
Women who suffer abuse in our neighbourhoods
and in the neighbourhood of the world.
Women who suffer while we look away, deny, remain silent.

We pray for those being crucified by disease,
by AIDS, TB, malaria …
Diseases which might be cured if only we'd choose life;
if only, as a world, we didn't spend over one trillion dollars U.S. a year
on bombs and bullets.

We pray for those being crucified in jails around the world,
in countries and by countries whose repressive governments
our government is happy to do business with
and to call good friends.

And we pray for this good earth we stand on,
this precious, fragile planet
we pay mock homage,
give poisoned streams to drink,
bind with fences,
strip and beat and flog,
pierce with spears until the blood and water pours out.

Jesus Christ,
we confess our complicity in all these crucifixions,
and in others.
Forgive us, Lord, we know not what we do.
Or do we?

We give thanks for individuals and organisations working
to bring healing and
hope in your world:

Church Action on Poverty
Oxfam
Save the Children
Christian Aid
Médecins Sans Frontières
Amnesty International
Earth First! …

(Invite pilgrims to call out names of other organisations in the world working to bring hope and healing.)

We give thanks for their passion and commitment.

Spirit of love, help us to do all that we can to support them in their work;
help us to do more to ease suffering and to bring healing and hope,
in our neighbourhoods and in the neighbourhood of the world.

Neil Paynter

Blessing

Christ of every suffering heart,
bless our awakening
as we begin to
discern more and more
your presence of life
within
the tortured
the abandoned
the persecuted
the imprisoned
the exploited
the betrayed
the violated
the abused
the silenced.

Peter Millar

SONGS

Goodness is stronger than evil (*Love and Anger,* Wild Goose Publications)
Kumbaya

NUNNERY (SEE PAGE 29)

JETTY

Each year, about 100,000 people visit Iona: pilgrims, guests of the different centres and houses of hospitality, volunteers, holidaymakers, day-trippers … Iona has been a place of pilgrimage for hundreds, probably thousands, of years. William Wordsworth, the Romantic poet, visited Iona, as did the politicians Donald Dewar and John Smith, who came here regularly, and is buried in the Reilig Odhráin. Leah Tutu, Desmond Tutu's wife, came in the 1980s to open the Iona Community's MacLeod Centre, and in the 1920s the Scottish Colourists came for a series of summers to paint in the village and down on the picturesque North Beach. Classical composer Felix Mendelssohn visited Iona (and Staffa, of course); rock 'n' roll stars have visited the island. Medieval pilgrims travelled to Iona seeking protection and healing, and modern-day seekers come searching for meaning and purpose …

In 1773, James Boswell and Dr Johnson visited Iona. In his journal, Boswell famously wrote:

When we had landed upon the sacred place, which, as long as I can remember, I had thought on with veneration, Dr Johnson and I cordially embraced. We had long talked of visiting Icolmkill; and, from the lateness of the season, were at times very doubtful whether we should be able to effect our purpose. To have seen it, even alone, would have given me great satisfaction; but the venerable scene was rendered much more pleasing by the company of my great and pious friend, who was no less affected by it than I was; and who has described the impressions it should make on the mind, with such strength of thought, and energy of language, that I shall quote his words, as conveying my own sensations much more forcibly than I am capable of doing: 'We are now treading that illustrious island, which was once the luminary of the Caledonian regions, whence savage clans and roving barbarians derived the benefits of knowledge, and the blessings of religion. To abstract the mind from all local emotion would be impossible if it were endeavoured, and would be foolish if it were possible. Whatever withdraws us from the power of our senses, whatever makes the past, the distant, or the future, predominate over the present, advances us in the dignity of thinking beings.

Far from me, and from my friends, be such frigid philosophy as may conduct us indifferent and unmoved over any ground which has been dignified by wisdom, bravery, or virtue. That man is little to be envied, whose patriotism would not gain force upon the plain of Marathon, or whose piety would not grow warmer among the ruins of Iona!'

From *The Journal of a Tour to the Hebrides with Samuel Johnson*, James Boswell

BIBLE READINGS

Let mutual love continue. Do not neglect to show hospitality to strangers, for by doing that some have entertained angels without knowing it.

Hebrews 13:1 (NRSV)

Psalm 121:7–8
Luke 24:13–35

REFLECTIONS

The jetty – a place of almost constant comings and goings, greetings and farewells – and the journey to and from Iona are often thought of metaphorically:

The journey

Steaming into the harbour at dusk,
wind ruffling the water and lights sliding under the waves.
A sense of coming home, familiar sounds:
cars revving, clanking up the ramp, disappearing with a flash of tail lights.
Hoisting our bags, their weight heavy on the shoulder.
Out into the dimness,
a few streetlights shining on wet tarmac.

Seaweed scenting the breeze, which shocks with its coldness.
The bus is waiting, engine running,
warmth inside against the night air.
Doors ease shut, we pull away.
A journey into the dark
yet not into the unknown.
I know every inch of the route.
The bumps and cattle grids,
the outlines of the glen, the colours of the hills,
the lochs reflecting in the fitful moonlight.
These dark hills are alive with heather.
In my mind the eagles swoop and soar,
turning and diving in the cool air.
The deer are running free
and otters fish for crabs.
I know each twist, each turn as well as my own hands.
This journey through the dark for me is filled with light.
Our bus, our bright-lit sanctuary, moves on, unstoppable.

And at the end, the lights are welcoming.
The dark waters of the Sound lap slowly round the ferry,
portals open, beckoning
as we board for
a final journey across dark waters.

And at the end?
The warmth of candles and the welcome of friends.
A sense of coming home.

Will it be like this on the final journey?
Crossing the Styx in a CalMac ferry
and waiting for the warmth of welcome?

Alix Brown

Jetty waking

Another little death:
a letting go
after the holding on
at the end of the jetty –
those clumsy hugs
and last words.

There will come a time
when you can't take
any of it with you;
but now, somehow,
you have to take it all:
bags, backpacks – all your stuff.

Another little death:
wading through the water
and, for those watching,
the ferry ramp closing
slowly, inexorably –
like curtains closing.

There will come a time
when we too will go this way:
crossing to the other side,
leaving the island of I.

But now, the world still asleep,
stand, salt spray stinging our eyes,
giving a good send-off, taking
leave, foolishly waving, weeping,
watching you out of sight, waking.

Jan Sutch Pickard

PRAYERS

An island in the sea

You are an island in the sea, O God,
you are a hill on the shore,
you are a star in the darkness,
you are a staff to the weak.

O, my soul's healer,
when I am lost and tired and stumbling
you shield and support me.
God, help me to give light, love and support to others.

Based on a prayer from the Carmina Gadelica

Prayer

As you were before us at our life's beginning,
be you so again at our journey's end.
As you were beside us at our soul's shaping,
God be also at our journey's close.

Iona Abbey Worship Book

SONGS

Mayenziwe (*Many and Great*, WGP)
The last journey (tune: 'Iona boat song') (*Enemy of Apathy*,
Wild Goose Publications)

MARTYRS' BAY

Martyrs' Bay was often used as a landing point for the island in the days before the current jetty was built, and was the place of arrival for the funeral corteges of many kings, chiefs and lords. Iona was considered an especially hallowed place for burial, and once ashore, coffins were rested on a nearby grassy knoll (which can be seen across the road, in the field at the head of the bay), before being processed up the 'Street of the Dead' for burial in the Reilig Odhráin. The other end of this medieval route can still be seen in the Abbey grounds today.

The bay takes its name from an event in 806, when, it is said, 68 monks were slaughtered at the hands of Viking invaders. The monastic community practised both hospitality and non-violence, and thus were an easy target for those with no such beliefs. Ultimately, the continuing Viking raids led to the Columban community eventually abandoning Iona and retreating to Ireland.

Nearby is the war memorial, commemorating the islanders who were killed in more recent wars. So perhaps here is a fitting place to remember all who die from violent acts; and to remember the contemporary martyrs who give their lives so that others may live free from fear and oppression.

BIBLE READINGS

Very truly, I tell you, unless a grain of wheat falls into the earth and dies, it remains just a single grain; but if it dies, it bears much fruit. Those who love their life lose it, and those who hate their life in this world will keep it for eternal life. Whoever serves me must follow me, and where I am, there will my servant be also.

John 12:24–26 (NRSV)

Matthew 5:38–45
Luke 21:14–18

REFLECTION

'[It says] in Christ's gospel that one must not love oneself so much as to avoid getting involved in the risks of life that history demands of us, and that those who try to fend off the danger will lose their lives, while those who out of love for Christ give themselves to the service of others, will live, live like the grain of wheat that dies, but only apparently. If it did not die, it would remain alone. The harvest comes about only because it dies, allowing itself to be sacrificed in the earth and destroyed. Only by undoing itself does it produce the harvest.'

From the last homily of Archbishop Oscar Romero, 24th March, 1980

PRAYER

Pray:

For peace in your country …

For victims of violence everywhere …

For those struggling for peace and justice …

For churches in conflict situations …

For a world without war and violence …

Lead us from death to life,
from falsehood to truth.
Lead us from despair to hope,
from fear to trust.
Lead us from hate to love,
from war to peace.
Let peace fill our hearts,
our world, our universe.
Amen

Universal prayer for peace

SONGS

Do not be afraid (G. Markland, *Church Hymnary 4*)
Na jijoho (*Sing with the World,* GIA Publications)

ERRATIC BOULDER

Just before the road turns the corner, down to the left can be seen a large (pink) boulder, perched incongruously upon the jagged rocks which compose this part of the shoreline. This sizeable chunk of granite is not native to Iona's foundations – it was carried here millions of years ago by the glaciers that covered much of Scotland during the last Ice Age. Needless to say, it has not moved since.

The rock came from Mull: there is no granite on Iona itself, apart from that washed up by the sea. If you took a boat a bit further down the coast, you would see some pink rocks sticking up out of the sea, which is where the granite ends, and the rocks that form Iona begin. The granite is around 800 million years old, while Iona is made up of some of the oldest rocks on the planet: Lewisian gneiss, which is around 2700 million years old, and Torridonian sandstone, a mere 1200 million years old. This explains why there are no fossils on Iona – complex organic life had not even begun at that point.

More 'recent' geological events (50 million years ago) can be seen in the terraced landscape of the Berg on Mull, and in the spectacular basalt columns that form the nearby island of Staffa, both formed by the action of long-dead volcanos.

Faced with the enormity of the timescale involved in forming this landscape, our lives can seem very small and brief indeed, as the words of Psalm 90 remind us:

BIBLE READINGS

Lord, you have been our dwelling-place
in all generations.

Before the mountains were brought forth,
or ever you had formed the earth and the world,
from everlasting to everlasting you are God.

You turn us back to dust,
and say, 'Turn back, you mortals.'
For a thousand years in your sight
are like yesterday when it is past,
or like a watch in the night.

You sweep them away; they are like a dream,
like grass that is renewed in the morning ...

Psalm 90:1–5 (NRSV)

Luke 19:39–40
1 Peter 2:4–10

PRAYER

God of all ages;
Jesus, yesterday, today and for ever;
Spirit breathing life since the dawn of creation;
give us courage to walk new paths with you;
open our eyes to the endless depth of your mystery.
Amen

Author unknown

SONGS

How can I keep from singing? (*I Will Not Sing Alone*, WGP)
Mungu mi mwema (*One Is the Body*, Wild Goose Publications)

CROSSROADS (SEE PAGE 39)

ON THE WAY

A wet pilgrimage

Yes, God
Yes!

I surrender myself
to this insistently penetrating rain
and through it …
I surrender myself
to you:

Saturate every part of me
with your life
       my thinking and speaking
       my willing and acting
       my loving and being.

Let nothing
remain dry …

Pat Bennett

MACHAIR

This stop is already covered in the off-road pilgrimage (see page 73). But for those taking the on-road version, this point on the route (being furthest away from the 'home comforts' of the village and the Abbey) is perhaps an appropriate stop at which to reflect on Columba's journey of exile, and his struggle to let go of his past. This is also a fitting place to carry out a symbolic action similar to the one traditionally performed at Columba's Bay: of casting a stone into the sea to represent that which we may need to leave behind, and taking one with us as we begin the return journey, to symbolise our commitment to a new way of being.

PRAYER

Letting go takes love

A: To let go does not mean to stop caring,
    it means I can't do it for someone else.

B: To let go is not to cut yourself off,
    it's the realisation I can't control another.

A: To let go is not to enable,
    but allow learning from natural consequences.

B: To let go is to allow powerlessness,
    which means the outcome is not in my hands.

A: To let go is not to try to change or blame another,
    it's to make the most of myself.

B: To let go is not to care for, but to care about.

A: To let go is not to fix, but to be supportive.

B: To let go is not to judge,
    but to allow another to be a human being.

A: To let go is not to be in the middle, arranging all the outcomes,
    but to allow others to affect their destinies.

B: To let go is not to be protective,
    it's to permit another to face reality.

A: To let go is not to deny, but to accept.

B: To let go is not to nag, scold or argue,
    but instead to search out my own shortcomings and correct them.

A: To let go is not to adjust everything to my desires,
    but to take each day as it comes and cherish myself in it.

B: To let go is not to criticise or regulate anybody,
    but to try to become what I dream I can be.

A: To let go is not to regret the past,
    but to grow and live for the future.

B: To let go is to fear less and love more.
    Remember: the time to love is short.

Attributed to Alcoholics Anonymous

HILL OF THE ANGELS (SEE PAGE 79)

HOUSE OF PRAYER (CNOC Á CHALMAIN)

This Roman Catholic retreat house was built in the 1990s, with the express purpose of furthering the cause of Christian unity through creating links with ecumenical work already happening on the island. It provides a place of prayer where people of all traditions are welcome to rest and to reflect. There are a number of Christian houses and places of worship on Iona (Bishop's House, the Parish Church …) In winter, worship is shared, and in summer worship is timed so that a visitor could participate in all the services on the island – if they chose!

BIBLE READINGS

'You are my friends if you do what I command … This is my command: Love each other.'

John 15:14,17 (NIV)

John 13:34–35
John 17:21–23

REFLECTION

Be patient toward all that is unsolved in your heart and try to love the questions themselves … Do not now seek answers, which cannot be given to you, because you would not be able to live them. And the point is, to live everything. Live the questions now. Perhaps you will gradually, without noticing it, live along some distant day into the answer.

Rainer Maria Rilke, from *Letters to a Young Poet*

PRAYERS

Draw us to Jesus, O God,
that we may draw closer
to each other.

Author unknown

In your love

God of our togetherness,
show me what we have in common,
when I can't see it for myself.

God of our sharing,
offer me what brings us ever closer,
even when I thought we were close enough already.

God of our communing,
show me what true communion means
with those who do things differently from me.

God of our connectedness,
show me how to strengthen our bonds,
especially when they threaten to break apart.

God of our understanding,
show me more of the mystery
which takes us beyond our limited knowledge.

God of our tiredness,
re-energise, restore and renew me
with your Spirit's unseen power.

God of our reluctance,
show me more of what is possible
with your way and in your love.

Tom Gordon

SONGS

Bind us together
How good and pleasant it is (*We Walk His Way*, Wild Goose Publications)

THE VILLAGE (BAILE MOR)

The village houses a busy community of about 100 people: there are B&Bs, hotels, shops, restaurants: all aspects of island hospitality. Other folk make their living from crofting, fishing, and taking visitors on boat trips to Staffa and around the islands. There are also gifted painters, potters, photographers, silversmiths, woodcarvers … There's a primary school, a doctor's surgery, a village hall, a library, a fire station …

The Heritage Centre, beside the parish church, is a wonderful place to spend some time learning about the story and spirit of the people of Iona, the true 'Iona community'. The history of habitation on Iona begins over ten thousand years ago in the Middle Stone Age and stretches through the Bronze Age, the Iron Age, the medieval period, the height of Gaelic culture, the creation of the crofts, the potato famine, the world wars … St Columba and Reverend George MacLeod are chapters of a much larger story that is still being lived.

It has been said that to learn the fuller, deeper, more grassroots history of a place, we must 'Ask the people who cut the hay.'[3]

BIBLE READINGS

Let love be genuine; hate what is evil, hold fast to what is good; love one another with mutual affection; outdo one another in showing honour. Do not lag in zeal, be ardent in spirit, serve the Lord. Rejoice in hope, be patient in suffering, persevere in prayer. Contribute to the needs of the saints; extend hospitality to strangers.

Romans 12:9–13 (NRSV)

Psalm 65:1, 9–13
Luke 10:38–42

PRAYERS

Your pattern of love

Loving God, we thank you for the gift of each other and of community. Help us to see and welcome you in all people and to dare to reach out to others no matter what the cost. Give us the courage to share our true selves. Teach us to live in harmony with all people, greeting your image within them and sharing their joys and sorrows. Bless the people of Iona and the people of the communities from which we come. Weave us together into your pattern of love. Amen

Author unknown

Jesus, who walked with farmers and fishers

Jesus, who walked with farmers and fishers
and sat in village kitchens,
walk with us now.

We hold before you those who have the privilege and responsibility
of working on the land and sea,
and those who struggle to make a living.

We hold before you those whose relationship with the earth is ruptured;
through conflict, poverty, stunted opportunities and environmental degradation.

We hold before you rural communities where people feel isolated, marginalised
and powerless in the face of distant economic and political forces.

We hold before you those whose policies affect the land, the earth and all of our lives;
and we pray for those in positions of power,
that they will have the courage and vision to make wise decisions.

God hear these prayers today
and fill us with your Spirit.
That we may live in peace with the earth
and with each other
and that your kingdom may come.

Jesus, who walked with farmers and fishers
and sat in village kitchens,
walk with us now.

Christian MacLean

Prayer

Be the eye of God dwelling with you,
the foot of Christ in guidance with you,
the shower of the Spirit pouring on you,
        richly and generously.
God's peace be to you,
Jesus' peace be to you,
the Spirit's peace be to you,
        and to your children;
aye, to you and your children,
each day and each night
of your portion in the world.
Amen

From the Carmina Gadelica

SONGS

God welcomes all (*We Walk His Way*, WGP)
The peace of the earth (*There Is One Among Us*, Wild Goose Publications)

REILIG ODHRÁIN (SEE PAGE 103)

(SEE PAGE 103)

ON THE WAY

On the road

I was a pilgrim
that summer
I went to Iona.

I slept in a tent
worshipped in an abbey
walked under stars.

I saw and heard God
in many new ways.

I went home
feeling good.

I went on living,
meeting God in new ways
in old places.

I was surprised.

Being a pilgrim
does something to you
that changes you forever.

It puts you
on the road
with God.

Ruth Burgess

Address to a pilgrim

Rome to Canterbury
Derry to Iona
Iona to Bamburgh
Bamburgh to Bradwell
Whitby to Whithorn –
pilgrimage is a circular route,
following the scuffmarks of history.

Beware the onslaught of nostalgia,
look out for sickly sentimentality,
the saintly monk who never broke a fingernail
or into sweat.
Remember, rather, and walk
in the footsteps of countless refugees,
tramping the forests of fear,
camping out in the fields of hopelessness;
the scent, not of crushed myrtle, but panic,
the sound, not of the lark, but of the sniper's bullet,
soaring, seeking warm flesh.

Seek then to remember
the brave steps of Mandela,
the unfinished work of Luther King,
the courage and compassion of Romero.
Carry with you also her-story:
Margaret of Scotland and Hilda of Whitby;
Clothilde and Bertha, persuasive princesses;

Elizabeth Fry and Emily Pankhurst,
who broke open prisons and set free prisoners.

Remember all the invisible ones;
walk in the footmarks of the forgotten ones.
And when your place of departure
becomes also your place of arrival
and you 'know the place for the first time'*
What has changed?
What have you indulged?
In seeking have you been found?
In penance have you travelled
the long hard road to restitution?
And as you step off and out of the procession,
what of you will those who continue
carry until you meet again?
What of them do you bring to us?

Kate McIlhagga

*T.S. Eliot

A PILGRIMAGE IN HAIKU

ST MARTIN'S CROSS

Sacred common life.
Divinely ordered pattern
of intertwining

THE NUNNERY

Tumbled broken walls.
Mute eloquent witnesses
to exclusion's wound.

MARTYRS' BAY

Ultimate asking.
A life, willingly given
from love … and with joy.

HILL OF ANGELS

Another seeing.
God's mysterious moments
penetrating flesh.

LOCH STAONAIG

Grasping hands offend
divine liberality.
Greed bleeds others dry.

MARBLE QUARRY

Eternal imprint,
vibrant throughout creation,
cannot be destroyed.

COLUMBA'S BAY

Hands slowly open,
letting go to grasp freedom's
possibilities.

THE MACHAIR

On the common ground
an accepting love flowers
to heal brokenness.

THE HERMIT'S CELL

Time evaporates.
Interior silence leads
to eternity.

DUN I

Mountaintop visions
can only be realised
on the downward path.

REILIG ODHRÁIN

In resurrection
God's ultimate paradox –
death liberates life.

Pat Bennett

SONGS

A NOTE ABOUT SINGING

For each of the pilgrimage stops we have included suggestions for a couple of songs or chants, four of which are included here. Like the other elements of this book, a song is not mandatory. However, singing can be a very useful and powerful addition to the pilgrimage, so a note of explanation:

Firstly, it's not a performance, so please don't worry if you don't consider yourself a singer. And belting out a number in your best 'West-End-musical' voice will only turn people into an audience. Beginning a song in the same way that you might sing 'Happy Birthday' to a loved friend is an invitation for others to join in, and form community – which is the purpose of these kind of songs.

Secondly, we have mostly suggested short songs, which can be repeated several times over, thus avoiding the need to have song sheets – which are not entirely compatible with Iona weather. Picking two or three such songs to use throughout the pilgrimage can be useful to mark the beginnings and endings of stops; to enable time for prayer and reflection; or simply to sing while the rest of the pilgrims catch up with you! They are particularly useful in gathering a group together. Rather than shouting at people to call them together for a reflection, it is perhaps more elegant to just begin a song, and repeat it until everyone is singing (and consequently, you have their attention for what comes next).

Finally, if you are using songs, it is worthwhile to teach them to the group at the beginning of the pilgrimage. Doing this not only helps to bring people together as a group, but also helps to ensure that everyone is on the 'inside' – there's nothing more exclusive than not knowing the song that everyone else is singing. Songs can be taught simply by singing a line at a time, and inviting everyone to repeat it, finishing up by singing the whole thing through together. The confidence with which you do this will be rewarded by a confident response from the group! Just imagine you're in the shower …

Happy singing!

KNOW THAT GOD IS GOOD (MUNGU NI MWEMA)

Melody: Democratic Republic of Congo, source unknown © copyright control.
Arrangement © Edo Bumba, Flöjtgatan 15, 42139 Västra Frölunda, Sweden
From One is the Body: Songs of Unity and Diversity, *John L. Bell, Wild Goose Publications, 2002*

BEHOLD, I MAKE ALL THINGS NEW

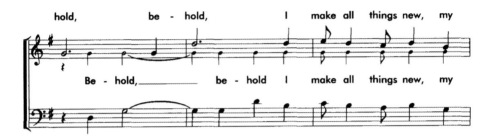

Behold, behold I make all things new,
beginning with you
and starting from today.
Behold, behold I make all things new,
my promise is true,
for I am Christ the way.

From Come All You People: Shorter Songs for Worship, John L. Bell, Wild Goose Publications, 1994

WE WILL WALK WITH GOD (SIZOHAMBA)

till   the   king - dom has come.
si - zo - ham - ba   na - ye.

Sizohamba naye
wo wo wo,
sizohamba naye. (Repeat)
Ngomhla wenjabula,
sizohamba naye. (Repeat)

We will walk with God, my brothers,
we will walk with God.
We will walk with God, my sisters,
we will walk with God.
We will go rejoicing, till the kingdom has come. *(Repeat)*

© Original words and music: Swaziland traditional, transcribed by the Swedish Youth Exchange project, 'Meeting Swaziland'. Translation by John L. Bell, © 2002 WGRG, Iona Community, Glasgow, Scotland
From One is the Body: Songs of Unity and Diversity, *John L. Bell, Wild Goose Publications, 2002*

SARANTAÑANI

BOLIVIA

positively and brightly

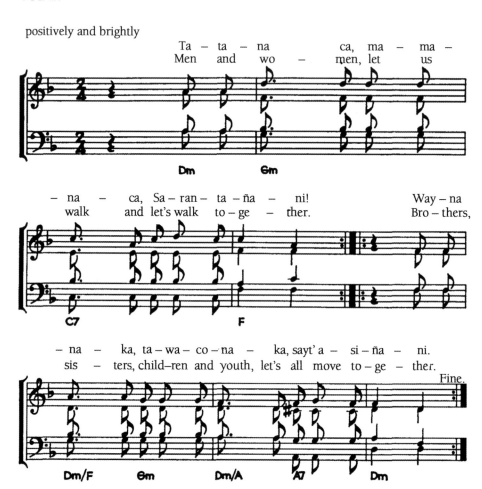

Tatanaca, mamanaca, Sarantañani!
Waynanaka, tawaconaka, sayt' asiñani.

Take Iglesia nacasaja mayaghasiñani,
Mayaqui, takeni, Sarantañani

Men and women, let us walk
and let's walk together.
Brothers, sisters, children and youth,
let's all move together.

Let the Church be one strong body,
walking together;
every member touched by each other,
keeping together.

N.B. The English translation is more of a paraphrase to prevent what might otherwise seem like bland words – something which would be an insult to the original.

The guitar chords are not totally consonant with the harmonised arrangement.

Words: © 1991 Zoilo Yanapa
Music: © 1991 Zoilo Yanapa;
              arrangement © 1991 Iona Community
From Sent by the Lord: Songs of the World Church, Vol. 2, Wild Goose Publications, John L. Bell

NOTES

1. 'What he conceived keeping vigil, by action he ascertained' – Thomas Clancy and Gilbert Márkus, *Iona: The Earliest Poetry of a Celtic Monastery*, Edinburgh University Press, 1995, p.113

2. The wording here is taken from a prayer written by Brian Woodcock, used in Iona Abbey.

3. The original quote is: 'Ask the fellows who cut the hay', and is from the poem 'The Decade of Sheng Min', translated by Ezra Pound; later used by George Ewart Evans in *Ask the Fellows Who Cut the Hay*, Faber, 1956

SOURCES AND ACKNOWLEDGEMENTS

Every effort has been made to trace copyright holders of all the items reproduced in this book. We would be glad to hear from anyone whom we have been unable to contact so that any omissions can be rectified in future editions.

'Setting out on the road' – by Dom Helder Camara, translated by Dinah Livingstone, from *The Desert is Fertile*, p.15, © 1974 Orbis Books. Used by permission of Orbis Books.

'The call' – John L. Bell and Graham Maule, from *Jesus and Peter*, John L. Bell and Graham Maule, Wild Goose Publications, © 1997 WGRG, Iona Community, Glasgow G2 3DH, Scotland.

'Disturber' – by Kate McIlhagga, from *The Green Heart of the Snowdrop*, Kate McIlhagga, Wild Goose Publications, 2004, © Donald McIlhagga.

'The Abbess's farewell' – by Mary Grey, from *Gathered and Scattered: Readings and Meditations from the Iona Community*, Neil Paynter (ed.), Wild Goose Publications, 2007. Used by permission of Mary Grey.

'When' – by Kathy Galloway, from *Talking to the Bones: Prayers and Meditations*, Kathy Galloway, SPCK, 1996. Used by permission of Kathy Galloway.

'I never wanted to be born' – by John L. Bell, from *He Was in the World: Meditations for Public Worship*, John L. Bell, Wild Goose Publications,1995, © 1995 WGRG, Iona Community, Glasgow G2 3DH, Scotland.

'Prescript' – by George MacLeod, from *Daily Readings with George MacLeod*, Ron Ferguson (ed.), Wild Goose Publications, 2004.

'Jacob's Luz becomes his Bethel' – by John Davies, from *Bare Feet and Buttercups: Resources for Ordinary Time – Trinity Sunday to the Feast of the Transfiguration*, Ruth Burgess (ed.), Wild Goose Publications, 2009.

'O Christ, you are within each of us …' – by George MacLeod, *Iona Abbey Worship Book*, Wild Goose Publications, 2001.

'Holy ground' – by Sandra Fox, from *Holy Ground: Liturgies and Worship Resources for an Engaged Spirituality*, Helen Boothroyd & Neil Paynter (eds), Wild Goose Publications, 2005.

'God in the thick of things and beyond (A house church at worship, Panama)' – by Ian M. Fraser, © Ian M. Fraser. Used by permission of Ian M. Fraser.

'Lord God, whose Son was content to die to bring new life …' – © Ian M. Fraser. Used by permission of Ian M. Fraser.

'Christ of every suffering heart' – by Peter Millar, from *A Book of Blessings*, Ruth Burgess (ed.), Wild Goose Publications, 2001.

'Jetty waking' – by Jan Sutch Pickard, from *Between High and Low Water: Sojourner Songs*, Jan Sutch Pickard, Wild Goose Publications, 2008.

'In your love' – by Tom Gordon, from *Gathered and Scattered: Readings and Meditations from the Iona Community*, Neil Paynter (ed.), Wild Goose Publications, 2007

'Jesus, who walked with farmers and fishers ...' – by Christian MacLean, from *Holy Ground: Liturgies and Worship Resources for an Engaged Spirituality*, Helen Boothroyd and Neil Paynter (eds), Wild Goose Publications, 2005.

'Be the eye of God dwelling with you' – from the *Carmina Gadelica*, Floris Books, 1992.

'Address to a pilgrim' – by Kate McIlhagga, from *The Green Heart of the Snowdrop*, Kate McIlhagga, Wild Goose Publications, 2004 © Donald McIlhagga.

OUTSIDE HOLINESS

Some resources and ideas for continuing the Iona pilgrimage out into the world ...

St Martin's Cross
Campaign Against the Arms Trade: www.caat.org.uk
Campaign for Nuclear Disarmament: www.cnduk.org
Shelter: www.shelter.org.uk
Trident Ploughshares: www.tridentploughshares.org
The Simon Community: www.simoncommunity.org.uk

The Nunnery
Coalition Against Trafficking in Women: www.catwinternational.org
Women's Aid: www.womensaid.org.uk
Women in Black: www.womeninblack.org.uk
Women's Resource Centre: www.wrc.org.uk

Marble Quarry
Friends of the Earth: www.foe.co.uk
Greenpeace: www.greenpeace.org.uk

Loch Staonaig
Christian Aid: www.christianaid.org.uk
WaterAid: www.wateraid.org/uk

Machair
Centre for Human Ecology: www.che.ac.uk
GalGael: www.galgael.org
Iona Community: www.iona.org.uk
L'Arche: www.larche.org.uk
The Soil Association: www.soilassociation.org
Traidcraft: www.traidcraft.co.uk

The Hermit's Cell
Contemplative Outreach: www.centeringprayer.com

Reilig Odhráin
Green funerals advice: http://tinyurl.com/greenfunerals

Parish Church
Church Action on Poverty: www.church-poverty.org.uk
Lesbian & Gay Christian Movement: www.lgcm.org.uk

MacLean's Cross
Amnesty International: www.amnesty.org.uk
Medical Foundation for the Care of Victims of Torture: www.torturecare.org.uk
Save the Children: www.savethechildren.org.uk

Martyrs' Bay
The Archbishop Romero Trust: www.romerotrust.org.uk

House of Prayer
CAFOD: www.cafod.org.uk
Pax Christi: www.paxchristi.org.uk/about.HTML
The Corrymeela Community: www.corrymeela.org
The Ecumenical Accompaniment Programme: www.eappi.org
The Open Door Community: www.opendoorcommunity.org
The Salvation Army: www2.salvationarmy.org.uk/uki/www_uki.nsf

Village

Isle of Gigha: www.gigha.org.uk
Mull and Iona Community Trust: www.mict.co.uk
Scottish Community Land Network: www.communityland.org.uk
The Isle of Eigg Heritage Trust: www.isleofeigg.net

BIBLIOGRAPHY

Adomnán's 'Law of the Innocents' – Cain Adomnán: A Seventh-century Law for the Protection of Non-Combatants, Gilbert Márkus, Kilmartin Museum, 2008

Advent Readings from Iona, Jan Sutch Pickard and Brian Woodcock, Wild Goose Publications, 2000

Against the Tide: The Story of Adomnán of Iona, Warren Bardsley, Wild Goose Publications, 2006

An Iona Anthology, F. Marian McNeill, New Iona Press, 1990

An Iona Prayer Book, Peter Millar, Canterbury Press, 1998

A Story to Live By, Kathy Galloway, SPCK, 1998

A Wee Worship Book, Wild Goose Resource Group, Wild Goose Publications, 1998

Between High and Low Water: Sojourner Songs, Jan Sutch Pickard, Wild Goose Publications, 2008

Celtic Christianity: Making Myths and Chasing Dreams, Ian Bradley, Edinburgh University Press, 1999

Chasing the Wild Goose: The Story of the Iona Community, Ron Ferguson, Wild Goose Publications, 1998

Christ of the Celts: The Healing of Creation, Philip Newell, Wild Goose Publications, 2009

Columba's Island: Iona from Past to Present, E. Mairi MacArthur, Edinburgh University Press, 1995

Columba: Pilgrim and Penitent, Ian Bradley, Wild Goose Publications, 1997

Daily Readings with George MacLeod, Ron Ferguson (ed.), Wild Goose Publications, 2004

De Locis Sanctis (On the Holy Places), Adomnán, (Scriptores Latini Hiberniae, Vol. 3), Dublin Institute for Advanced Studies, 1958

Essays in Commemoration of the Law of the Innocents, Thomas O'Loughlin (ed.), Four Courts Press, 2001

Every Blessed Thing: An Evening with George MacLeod, Tom Fleming and Ron Ferguson, Wild Goose Publications, 2005

Flowers of Iona, Jean M. Millar, New Iona Press, 1993

Gathered and Scattered: Readings and Meditations from the Iona Community, Neil Paynter (ed.), Wild Goose Publications, 2007

George MacLeod: A Biography, Ron Ferguson, Wild Goose Publications, 2004

Growing Hope: Daily Readings, Neil Paynter (ed.), Wild Goose Publications, 2006

Holy Ground: Liturgies and Worship Resources for an Engaged Spirituality, Helen Boothroyd and Neil Paynter (eds), Wild Goose Publications, 2005

Inventory of the Ancient Monuments: Argyll Vol. 4, Royal Commission on the Ancient and Historical Monuments of Scotland, 1982

Iona, Anna Ritchie, Historic Scotland/Batsford, 1997

Iona (Colin Baxter Island Guides), E. Mairi MacArthur and Iain Sarjeant, Colin Baxter, 2001

Iona Abbey: A Pilgrim's Guide, Chris Polhill, Wild Goose Publications, 2006

Iona Abbey Music Book, Wild Goose Publications, 2002

Iona Abbey Worship Book, Wild Goose Publications, 2001

Iona: A Map, Iona Community (available from the Iona Community Shop, www.iona.org.uk)

Iona and Staffa (video/DVD), script by E. Mairi MacArthur, Video Highland Productions, 2001

Iona Celtic Art: The Work of Alexander and Euphemia Ritchie, New Iona Press, 2003

Iona: Dove across the Water (film), director, Mike Alexander, Films of Scotland (see the Scottish Screen Archive website)

Iona – God's Energy: The Spirituality and Vision of the Iona Community, Norman Shanks, Wild Goose Publications, 2009

Iona: Images and Reflections, David Coleman and Neil Paynter, Wild Goose Publications, 2007

Iona, Kells and Derry, Maire Herbert, Four Courts Press, 1996

Iona: Pilgrim Guide, Peter Millar, illustrations by Gordon Menzies, Canterbury Press, 1997

Iona: Poems, Kenneth C. Steven, St Andrew Press, 2000

Iona Portrayed: The Island through Artists' Eyes 1790-1960, Jessica Christian and Charles Stiller, New Iona Press, 2000

Iona, Staffa and Ross of Mull Ordnance Survey Explorer Map Active, Ordnance Survey, 2007

Iona: The Earliest Poetry of a Celtic Monastery, Thomas Owen Clancy and Gilbert Márkus, Edinburgh University Press, 1995

Iona: The Living Memory of a Crofting Community, E. Mairi MacArthur, Polygon, 1990

Life of St Columba (trans. Richard Sharpe), Adomnán of Iona, Penguin Classics, 2005

Living a Countersign: From Iona to Basic Christian Communities, Ian M. Fraser, Wild Goose Publications (Iona Community Classics Series), 1990, 2008

Living by the Rule: The Rule of the Iona Community, Kathy Galloway, Wild Goose Publications, 2010

Only One Way Left, George MacLeod, Wild Goose Publications (Iona Community Classics Series), 1954, 2005

Out of Iona: Words from a Crossroads of the World, Jan Sutch Pickard, Wild Goose Publications, 2003

Pilgrimage: A Spiritual and Cultural Journey, Ian Bradley, Lion Publishing, 2009

Pilgrimage in Medieval Scotland, Peter Yeoman, Historic Scotland/Batsford, 1999

Studies in the Cult of Saint Columba, C. Bourke (ed.), Four Courts Press, 1997

Talking to the Bones: Prayers and Meditations, Kathy Galloway, SPCK, 1996

That Illustrious Island: Iona through Travellers' Eyes, E. Mairi MacArthur (ed.) New Iona Press, 1991

The Carmina Gadelica: Hymns and Invocations, Alexander Carmichael, Floris, 1992

The Celtic Quest: A Contemporary Spirituality, Rosemary Power, The Columba Press, 2010

The Cloisters of Iona Abbey, Ewan Mathers, Wild Goose Publications, 2001

The Dream of Learning our True Name, Kathy Galloway, Wild Goose Publications, 2004

The Ethic of Traditional Communities and the Spirit of Healing Justice: Studies from Hollow Water, the Iona Community, and Plum Village, Jarem Sawatsky, Jessica Kingsley Publishers, 2009

The Guide to Mysterious Iona and Staffa, Geoff Holder, Tempus, 2007

The Iona Community: Today's Hope, Tomorrow's Challenge/Sermon in Stone (DVD), Wild Goose Publications, 1998

The Isle of Iona: Sacred, Spectacular, Living, Alastair De Watteville, 1998

The Journey Home (the story of the return of the original St John's Cross to Iona) (video), Iona Cathedral Trustees, 1991 (hard to find)

The Lonely Gannet's Pocket Guide to Iona, Gordon Bruce, Lonely Gannet, 2008

The Marble Quarry, D.J. Viner, New Iona Press, 1992

The Pattern of Our Days: Liturgies and Resources for Worship from the Iona Community, Kathy Galloway (ed.), Wild Goose Publications, 1996

The Whole Earth Shall Cry Glory: Iona Prayers, George MacLeod, Wild Goose Publications, 1985, 2007

This Is the Day: Readings and Meditations from the Iona Community, Neil Paynter (ed.), Wild Goose Publications, 2002

Waymarks: Signposts to Discovering God's Presence in the World, Peter Millar, Canterbury Press, 1998

For other related books and downloads, including many of the songbooks by John Bell and Graham Maule referenced in this book, see www.ionabooks.com

PHOTO CREDITS

Photos on pages 54, 58 and 59, 65, 77, 81, 86, 95, 96, 120, 127, 132, 140, 151, 156, 160, 164 and 168, and cover photo by Anja Grosse-Uhlmann

Photos on pages 14, 16, 20, 30, 38, 44, 49, 50, 73, 104, 113, 144, 147, 178 and 183 by David Coleman

Photo on page 6 by Michelle Harris

Photo on page 8 by ©iStockphoto.com/John Butterfield

Photos on pages 1, 3, 5 and 63 ©iStockphoto.com/Alexandr Labetskiy

WILD GOOSE PUBLICATIONS IS PART OF THE IONA COMMUNITY:

- An ecumenical movement of men and women from different walks of life and different traditions in the Christian church
- Committed to the gospel of Jesus Christ, and to following where that leads, even into the unknown
- Engaged together, and with people of goodwill across the world, in acting, reflecting and praying for justice, peace and the integrity of creation
- Convinced that the inclusive community we seek must be embodied in the community we practise

Together with our staff, we are responsible for:

- Our islands residential centres of Iona Abbey, the MacLeod Centre on Iona, and Camas Adventure Centre on the Ross of Mull

and in Glasgow:

- The administration of the Community
- Our work with young people
- Our publishing house, Wild Goose Publications
- Our association in the revitalising of worship with the Wild Goose Resource Group

The Iona Community was founded in Glasgow in 1938 by George MacLeod, minister, visionary and prophetic witness for peace, in the context of the poverty and despair of the Depression. Its original task of rebuilding the monastic ruins of Iona Abbey became a sign of hopeful rebuilding of community in Scotland and beyond. Today, we are about 250 Members, mostly in Britain, and 1500 Associate Members, with 1400 Friends worldwide. Together and apart, 'we follow the light we have, and pray for more light'.

For information on the Iona Community contact:
The Iona Community, Fourth Floor, Savoy House, 140 Sauchiehall Street, Glasgow G2 3DH,
UK. Phone: 0141 332 6343
e-mail: admin@iona.org.uk; web: www.iona.org.uk

For enquiries about visiting Iona, please contact:
Iona Abbey, Isle of Iona, Argyll PA76 6SN, UK. Phone: 01681 700404
e-mail: ionacomm@iona.org.uk